CONVERSATIONAL BIBLE STUDIES

New Testament

CONVERSATIONAL BIBLE STUDIES

New Testament

JAMES A. SCHACHER

CONTEMPORARY DISCUSSION SERIES

BAKER BOOK HOUSE
Grand Rapids, Michigan

CONTENTS

INTRODUCTION

What is one of the most stimulating experiences in the Christian life? Bible study! Especially Bible study in conversation with fellow believers.

Bible study groups have taken many different formats in our society. Neighborhood Bible studies, especially those sponsored by local churches, are multiplying. Some industries allow groups to meet for this purpose in their plants. Athletic teams and campus organizations sponsor prayer and Bible sharing hours.

A wealth of Bible study material is available. There are Bible studies for daily devotions in the home, for specific situations such as hospitalizations, and for particular age groups. However, there is very little material available for a conversational study of the Bible which is firmly grounded in the text. The studies in this book are intended to fill this need.

Two steps are essential in a conversational Bible study: securing information and group discussion. There is also a third step included in each of the studies in this book—research questions. This is the format of each New Testament study in this book: information, discussion, and research. The first two steps, securing information and group discussion, should both be done by the Bible study group when they meet together, and the third step, the research questions, should be done by individual group members at another time.

The first section of each study, titled **Basic Information** and based on the King James Version of the Bible, helps the group to discover elementary data. Many people do not begin Bible study because it seems so difficult and mysterious. However, if we use *who, what, where,* and *when* questions in conjunction with several translations of the Bible, we can begin a countdown toward the facts. In other words, we can find out what the text says.

The **Discussion and Application** section of each study helps the group to look to the Bible for insights into personal needs and to stimulate them toward a more creative approach to living in our society. Unfortunately, some existing materials emphasize relational theology to the neglect of the Biblical text. Truth should arise out of the Bible rather than being injected into it. Otherwise religion merely reflects what is already in the world. The aim, then, is to avoid exercises in psychology which could just as well be conducted in a therapy group not based on Christian presuppositions.

Each Bible study also contains a section titled **Additional Research**. It deals with matters which go beyond what is stated in the text. Textual exegesis, Biblical theology, and systematic theology are involved in these questions. The questions are similar to outside assignments in the classroom. Reference works such as Bible atlases, dictionaries, concordances, and commentaries, along with detailed comparison of cross-references within the Bible, afford opportunities to channel extra energy. Obviously, with four to seven questions per study, these research questions are not exhaustive. However, they can serve to broaden the horizon of the serious student.

The sections of research questions are placed after the first two sections in each study because the research is based on the material already discovered in the earlier sections. However, this research could be done individually by group members before the group discussion, and this would add meaningful background and substance to the discussion.

After all or part of a New Testament book has been examined in a series of studies, there follows a section titled **Reflections**. This section constitutes more than a review. It does reiterate selected ideas, but it also attempts to expose patterns and to transcend the verse-by-verse approach of each study.

Each of these four sections is offered as a vehicle to begin the adventure of discovering God's Word. No matter what method of study we may prefer or what our present station in life may be, all of us need to study God's Word. These studies can assist us in many of the situations we experience in our Christian lives.

Personal devotions may be dynamic or dragging. Discipline in this area is difficult for many Christians to attain. How can we begin anew after we have been neglecting devotions? How can we keep our minds from wandering during devotions? We should always have an objective while reading a Bible passage, and a series of questions, such as those found in these studies, can provide such direction. These studies should help individuals establish good habits in private worship.

Sunday school teachers, too, could sharpen their skills with the use of these studies. They will encourage the teacher systematically to study the Scripture passage in the Sunday school lesson and even to incorporate these study methods in the weekly lesson. For example, applying the Bible to home, school, church, and society, as in the Discussion and Application sections, could be used in the application of the Sunday school lesson. The method of tying together details in the Reflections section of these studies could also be used to show a broader view of the Bible. Instead of seeing only individual snapshots each Sunday, the class could see the Bible as a panorama and a whole.

Finally, these studies are intended as the foundation for dynamic sharing groups. Human relations are often cold and impersonal in our computer age. Even Christians forfeit a vital dimension of their fellowship. Many Christians hurt inside, but they seem to be afraid of exposing their real selves to one another. As a result they wear masks. They sit side by side in pews week after week and never discover one another. These Christians haven't learned that the Holy Spirit wishes to use someone's warm hand and understanding ear to minister to them. Nor are they aware that they should be caring for someone else. When this awareness develops, the Christian's sensitivity will lift off and rise above the levels of weather, sports, and babies. The Christian will begin to deal more effectively with attitudes and feelings—where real living takes place.

Some may object that the Discussion and Application questions become too personal. That may be correct in some cases. Naturally, study groups must use discretion. Baring the soul is seldom wise, but more often the error lies in remaining too abstract and out of touch with the practical interests of Scripture.

It would be wise for each study group to discuss and agree on basic guidelines. Here are a number of suggestions for group Bible studies:

1. Divide large groups into smaller units of five or six people.
2. Groups should meet regularly for a designated number of weeks or months.
3. Each group should covenant to give their

meetings priority over other activities and to be punctual.

4. Groups should pray. At the beginning of each session they should ask for the Holy Spirit's direction. Members should pray each day for everyone in the group.

5. It is very helpful for each group member to have written a personal reaction or opinion to a topic related to the lesson before trying to begin the group discussion. This should not be presented as a requirement, but as an opportunity to search the Scripture passage and to stimulate discussion. The benefit we realize from this exercise will depend upon how much we have put into it.

6. The discussion should not focus on the faults of others, but rather on "how I feel and how I need to improve." Focusing on personal needs will counteract the tendency to gossip.

7. Don't overemphasize the ideal in the discussions. Usually, we already know what we should do; we need the motivation to do it.

8. Be honest. Quit pretending. God knows anyhow. Deal with real life.

9. Be free—share God's gift of personality with fellow group members. However, we must also accept the opinions and outlooks of others. We can't expect others to accept us if we don't accept them.

10. Be loving. Don't be afraid to express compassion and to be understanding. You will never know how meaningful this is until you undergo a trying experience yourself.

11. Don't make others feel they must talk or share if they are not ready.

12. Trust and responsibility within each group must be developed. As one shares his personal life, he can discover if others in the group are

supportive and trustworthy. As a few members of the group lower their masks and deal more with their real needs, others will feel more free to respond. The group will begin to realize that when a group member shares part of his personal life, he is giving the others a sacred trust. This, in turn, builds responsibility and character within group members.

Well, that is the plan. Now what? Some Christians testify that when they first discovered the thrill of God's voice speaking to them through the Bible, it was like the effervescence that pops and bursts outward when a soft drink can is opened. This might not describe your experience, but, however it happens, may He touch you where you think and feel and live. This is what it means to know the eternal life which the new birth provides (I John 5:1, 13).

1

MARK

The Beginning of Jesus' Ministry
Chapters 1—4

STUDY 1: MARK 1:1-8

BASIC INFORMATION

1. How is Jesus described in v. 1?
2. Where did John the Baptist preach? Can you locate the place on a map?
3. What prediction did John have about the "mightier" one who was to come?

DISCUSSION AND APPLICATION

1. Compare vss. 7–8 with Matthew 3:7–8. Then write what John the Baptist would tell:
   (a) derelicts on skid row
   (b) a lady on the society register in Washington, D.C.
   (c) a businessman operating a discount store
2. What sermons have you heard which are similar in tone to John the Baptist's?
3. Suggest some ways in which Americans could repent of their sins. How could your community

change? How could your church improve? How about you yourself?

4. List some excuses that believers often give for not witnessing as boldly as John the Baptist. Evaluate these reasons to see if any are valid.

ADDITIONAL RESEARCH

1. How many words can you find in this passage which end in the letters *ing*? (Use several translations.) Why did Mark use them? Is any special understanding of Jesus' life made clear to us as a result?

2. Define *repentance*. Use a Bible concordance. Then refer to a Bible dictionary or a book on doctrine.

3. What does it mean to be "baptized with the Holy Ghost"? (Cf. Acts 1:5, 8; 11:16; 13:3; 19:6; I Corinthians 12:13; Romans 8:9; and others.)

4. Explain what "baptism of repentance for the remission of sins" means.

5. Which Old Testament prophets were like John the Baptist in personality and ministry?

STUDY 2: MARK 1:9–13

BASIC INFORMATION

1. List four things which Jesus experienced in vss. 10–11.

2. Can you find five living beings mentioned in vss. 12–13?

3. What was the Father's attitude toward the Son?

4. Who sent Jesus into the desert?
5. What does this passage reveal about the activity of angels?

DISCUSSION AND APPLICATION

1. Imagine that you were present at Jesus' baptism. Describe what the setting may have been. What mood does this create? If you were an artist, what features would you include when painting this scene?
2. If no one had ever explained vss. 10–11 to you, how would you interpret them? How necessary was Jesus's baptism, in your opinion?
3. What temptation have you experienced which seemed as intense as Satan's temptation of Jesus?
4. If you had observed Jesus' glorious baptism, would you be more capable of overcoming temptation? Would it have improved your faith?
5. How does baptism differ from initiation into a club or fraternity?
6. In relation to v. 11, what can *we* do which would please the Father?

ADDITIONAL RESEARCH

1. How does Jesus' baptism differ from His transfiguration?
2. Is there evidence for the doctrine of the Trinity in vss. 9–13?
3. Is one of the purposes of Jesus' baptism to accredit Him as God's messenger?
4. How many verbs and adverbs in this passage denote urgent action?
5. Find the references in Matthew and Luke which

report Jesus' temptation in the wilderness. How is Mark's account different? Similar? What was the evil in the first two temptations?

6. This baptism was recorded from the viewpoint of:
   (a) Jesus' observations
   (b) a bystander's observations
   (c) the Heavenly Father's observations

7. Can you find another reference to the Father designating Jesus as His beloved Son in one of the New Testament epistles?

STUDY 3: MARK 1:14–20

BASIC INFORMATION

1. Where was Jesus preaching when He called His disciples?

2. What message was He preaching? What did He tell the people to do?

3. Reword v. 15. You might want to express it as if you were one of the following:
   (a) an athletic coach addressing his players
   (b) a housewife speaking to her children
   (c) a visitor at the side of a dying relative

4. How long did it take Simon and Andrew to follow Jesus?

DISCUSSION AND APPLICATION

1. If people today were to repent, how would that change their life style?

2. In vss. 17–18 Simon and Andrew followed Jesus. What attracts you to follow Christ?

3. Instead of talking to fishermen in boats, imagine that Jesus is walking into a business office today, and that He calls an executive and several secretaries to follow Him. Instead of saying that He would make them "fishers of men," what might He tell them? How would He address a construction foreman, a photographer's model, a photographer, a teacher, or a seamstress?
4. What task is God calling you to do?

ADDITIONAL RESEARCH

1. Define *kingdom, gospel, fishers of men.*
2. What can you learn about Zebedee from this passage and in other places where he or his sons are mentioned?
3. In what way did His temptation prepare Jesus to go out and call these men to follow him?
4. Research the method of fishing in that day. What was the relationship between their labor and their economic standing in the community?

STUDY 4: MARK 1:21–45

BASIC INFORMATION

1. What was unusual about Jesus' teaching?
2. Describe the emotions of the demon. Why did he feel like that?
3. What other people did Jesus heal? What were their afflictions?
4. What was Jesus' attitude toward the leper?
5. Outline this passage. (List the main events and the verses in which they are found.)

DISCUSSION AND APPLICATION

1. Why were the people amazed at Jesus? How would you feel if you encountered someone like that today?

2. What books and movies on demon possession have you seen advertised? Is this a legitimate subject for the secular media to explore?

3. Have you ever been healed? Do you know someone who has? What is your evaluation of faith healing?

4. How is Jesus' approach different from Dr. Spock's?

5. If the needy do not receive an immediate answer to prayer, is there still some encouragement for them in this passage?

6. How could Jesus' prayer life influence your prayer time?

ADDITIONAL RESEARCH

1. What were the physical, social, emotional, and ceremonial results of leprosy?

2. On what other occasions did Jesus cast out demons?

3. What is the *wholeness* concept of healing? How is it illustrated in this passage?

4. Read the incident involving leprosy victims in the book, *Ben Hur*. Is it overdramatized?

STUDY 5: MARK 2:1–12

BASIC INFORMATION

1. Where did this event take place?

2. What was the goal of the sick man's friends?

3. Describe the reactions and motives of the scribes.
4. Choose the key verse in this passage.
5. Retell the story in sixty seconds.

DISCUSSION AND APPLICATION

1. Pretend that you were the owner of this house. How would you have reacted to this incident?
2. Why did Jesus' action disturb the Pharisees?
3. What were Jesus' feelings when He was doubted? How would you have felt?
4. Would you make a public spectacle of yourself to help a friend with cancer? Is there something else you could do to help someone today?
5. Which statement concerning Jesus' power to forgive sins is most correct:
   (a) Jesus was aware that he couldn't forgive sins and so He deliberately deceived people. Therefore He could not have been a good man.
   (b) Jesus actually thought He could forgive sins, but was not able to do it. So He must have been under delusions of grandeur and was not a wise teacher.
   (c) Jesus did have power to forgive sins and is our only access to heaven (John 10). Therefore He is God and has the authority to direct our lives.
6. How does your response to the previous question affect your way of life? Your attitudes?

ADDITIONAL RESEARCH

1. Jesus told the healed man to go home. Make a list of the instructions which He gave to people who were healed on other occasions.
2. Define *blasphemy*.

3. Find the verses in which these topics are alluded to: *second-guessing, sacrilege, education.* Can you find other subjects which are suggested in this passage?
4. What is the relationship between healing and forgiveness of sins in this passage?
5. What were some other events in Jesus' ministry which occurred at Capernaum?

STUDY 6: MARK 2:13–28

BASIC INFORMATION

1. With what charges did the Pharisees challenge Jesus?
2. Why did Jesus say that He was friendly toward the ungodly?
3. What is the main truth taught in vss. 18–22?
4. Correct this statement: "Man was made for the sabbath and not the sabbath for man." Explain the meaning of the corrected statement.
5. Choose a heading for each of these paragraphs: vss. 15–17; vss. 18–22; vss. 23–28.
6. How does the idea of new wine in old wineskins relate to the dialogue in vss. 18–20?

DISCUSSION AND APPLICATION

1. "Jesus is a killjoy." Can you find evidence here to support or oppose this statement? How does this evidence compare to the impression that many people have of Jesus?
2. What are some pitfalls for Christians to avoid when they befriend unbelievers?

3. Can people misinterpret v. 27 to justify their misuse of Sunday?
4. Do these verses give you some instruction which you must strive to achieve?
5. How are the Pharisees like some sensational newspaper columnists?
6. What old garments are Christians wearing today which they could discard?

ADDITIONAL RESEARCH

1. What are some differences between the scribes and the Pharisees?
2. Trace the growth of opposition from 1:1 to 3:6.
3. Find the passage in the Old Testament referred to in vss. 25–26.
4. In what way are the three incidents within this passage related?
5. What light is shed here on the relationship of the law and the gospel?

STUDY 7: MARK 3:1–19

BASIC INFORMATION

1. What was the man's handicap in this story?
2. Did Jesus consider it acceptable to heal on Sunday?
3. What emotions do the different individuals display in vss. 1–6?
4. State the demons' opinion of Jesus (v. 11). How did they act?
5. For what purpose did Jesus select the twelve?

DISCUSSION AND APPLICATION

1. Imagine that you were in the group in v. 6. What do you suppose was said in the conversation?
2. Do you identify with Jesus or the Pharisees? Do the Pharisees always seem to lose, like the court opponents of Perry Mason? Can you recall when you acted as Jesus did here? As the Pharisees did?
3. Have you ever been at a worship service held on a beach? How was it different than the average indoor church service?
4. If Jesus were to summon you to leave your job and community where you are living, what would be your reaction? Does He have the right to interfere with your plans? What excuses automatically surface? Everything considered, what would you do?

ADDITIONAL RESEARCH

1. Who were the Herodians?
2. Utilizing a Bible dictionary or a source explaining the New Testament Greek, differentiate between:
   (a) a miracle
   (b) a wonder
   (c) a sign
3. Would it have been better to include vss. 1–6 in the same study as 2:23–28? Why were they placed in different chapters?
4. Define *hardness of heart.* Has your heart ever been hardened? What can soften a hard heart?
5. How does this list of the twelve disciples compare to lists in the other gospels?

STUDY 8: MARK 3:20–35

BASIC INFORMATION

1. Why did Jesus' friends become concerned about Him?
2. Match the passages in the columns on the left with the opinions in the column on the right:
   Mark 3:20–21   the scribes' opinion of Jesus
   Mark 3:31–35   Jesus' friends' opinion of Him
   Mark 3:22–30   Jesus' opinion of His family
3. Explain the logic of vss. 24–26.
4. How does v. 28 answer the charge in v. 22?
5. Who is Jesus' brother?

DISCUSSION AND APPLICATION

1. Why do friends sometimes misunderstand each other (cf. v. 21)?
2. Can you give an illustration from the world of business, finance, or sports which supports the point in v. 25?
3. "The sin against the Holy Spirit is terrible because one who rejects the enlightenment of the Spirit has no other avenue of repentance." True or false? Why?
4. Did Jesus' comment in this passage cast a bad reflection on the family in which He grew up?
5. How can you do a better job of doing God's will in the next twenty-four hours? Do you think that you would feel closer to Jesus as a result?

ADDITIONAL RESEARCH

1. How are vss. 22–30 related to I John 5:16?
2. What sins apparently can be forgiven in the light of v. 28?

3. What are the implications regarding Mary, the mother of Jesus, from vss. 31–35?
4. Why aren't Jesus' father or sisters mentioned in v. 31?

STUDY 9: MARK 4:1–20

BASIC INFORMATION

1. On what occasion did Jesus speak the parable of the sower?
2. Are there four or five kinds of soil which Jesus described? List them.
3. What is the purpose of using parables according to vss. 11–12? What do these verses mean?
4. *Satan*, the *world*, and inner desires (*lusts*) are all said to play a role in counteracting the effect of God's Word. Reread the verses in which each of these elements is discussed. Is there another New Testament passage which refers to all three?
5. What results from seed planted on good ground?

DISCUSSION AND APPLICATION

1. Suppose that you planted a flower garden. You tended it carefully, but blossoms failed to appear. How would you feel?
2. "The wealthiest people in our church are the ones most likely to be overcome by the cares of this world." True or false? What is the other side of the coin?
3. Which kind of soil does your life most closely resemble?

4. Does this passage offer encouragement to pastors or laymen who see few results from their witnessing? Could it become an excuse for failure? How?
5. How would a farmer raise his crop if he were faced with some of the problems in this passage? How can Christians cope with spiritual afflictions like this?

ADDITIONAL RESEARCH

1. At what stage of His ministry was this parable of the sower spoken by Jesus?
2. How is this parable related to the other parables in this chapter?
3. Can you find different interpretations of vss. 11–12 from outside sources?
4. What does this parable reveal about the kingdom of God, the concept of eternal security, the free will of man, God's plan for the world, and Satan?

STUDY 10: MARK 4:21–34

BASIC INFORMATION

1. What is the purpose of light? What verse answers this question?
2. What will someday be revealed according to this passage?
3. How is the kingdom of heaven like wheat which is harvested?
4. How is the kingdom of heaven like a tiny seed which grows into a large tree?

5. What did Jesus do when He was alone with the disciples?

DISCUSSION AND APPLICATION

1. In what way is your light hidden?
2. Do many, some, or few people have things in their lives to hide? Will this all some day be made public?
3. If your life were to be harvested now, what would be the result:

   (a) You would have a bumper crop.
   (b) You would have an average yield.
   (c) You would barely be able to meet expenses.
   (d) You would go bankrupt.
4. Can you recall an instance in which you understood God's will more, after you had begun to obey Him (v. 24)?
5. "The idea of harvesting in this passage is used because Jesus wished to emphasize the idea of punishment." Do you agree or not? Why?

ADDITIONAL RESEARCH

1. What is the difference between the church and the kingdom of heaven?
2. What scientific methods does a farmer use today in an effort to make his business profitable? Do these methods illustrate Christian truths?
3. How large is a mustard seed compared to other seeds?
4. Explain the economics described in v. 25.

STUDY 11: MARK 4:35–41

BASIC INFORMATION

1. At what time of day did Jesus and His disciples decide to cross the lake?
2. What was Jesus doing during the first part of the storm?
3. How did the other passengers act?
4. What two statements did Jesus make?
5. What did the people conclude about Jesus after He had calmed the storm?

DISCUSSION AND APPLICATION

1. How would you have felt if you had been in the boat during the storm? Have you ever found yourself in that type of predicament?
2. What are some things that create fear within people you know? What fear do you have regarding your family, for instance?
3. If you had seen Jesus stop the wind, would that help you believe that He would help you in your problems?
4. If Jesus did control the winds and the waves, what would that prove?
5. Have you or people in your church had a definite answer to prayer recently?
6. Can you recall a time when you had a distinct feeling of awe and reverence for God?

ADDITIONAL RESEARCH

1. Look up this incident in the other gospels and compare the accounts.
2. Make a list of Jesus' miracles which affected nature (other than healings).

3. Read Psalm 46 and then write a psalm of your own. Incorporate elements of vss. 35–41, Psalm 46, and some specific experiences of your own.

REFLECTIONS ON MARK

1. List Jesus' deeds of kindness recorded in these chapters.
2. How many miracles did Jesus perform in Mark 1–4?
3. Can you cite chapter and verse to illustrate Mark's peculiar emphasis upon immediate action?
4. Some say that Mark uniquely presents Jesus as the suffering servant. Do these four chapters support that idea?
5. What attracts you to Jesus? Is there something about Christ which makes you feel that He has the answers to the riddles in your life?
6. What made you feel that Jesus was a real, living man who lived in Palestine and walked its dusty roads 2000 years ago?
7. Did you encounter any evidence in Mark that would support the view that Jesus is God?
8. Which one of the parables applied most to your life?

2

LUKE

The Close of Jesus' Teaching Ministry
Chapters 18—21

STUDY 1: LUKE 18:1–8

BASIC INFORMATION

1. What was the widow's request?
2. Describe the character of the judge.
3. Why did he finally grant the widow's request?
4. What is the main truth this story teaches?

DISCUSSION AND APPLICATION

1. Are you more like the judge or the widow? Do you know other people who are like either of them?
2. If you were sure that your repeated prayers would be answered, how would that affect your prayer life? How can you begin today to improve your prayer life?
3. In nineteenth century England, George Muller directed an orphanage without requesting financial aid from anyone but God. Does this example illustrate the truth of this passage?

4. How could church prayer meetings be improved according to this passage?
5. Does this motivate you to be more consistent in praying at a certain time and place each day?
6. Make a list of things for which you could continue to pray until God had responded.

ADDITIONAL RESEARCH

1. Is it a problem to understand how an unrighteous judge can be compared to God?
2. What other verses in Luke tell about Jesus' dealings with a widow?
3. What is revealed about the second coming of Christ in v. 8? How does that fit into the rest of the passage?
4. How does v. 5 compare to Matthew 6:7–8?

STUDY 2: LUKE 18:9–17

BASIC INFORMATION

1. Where did the two men go? Why did they go there?
2. What kind of a person was the Pharisee? The publican?
3. Why did Jesus tell this story? Find the verse that tells why.
4. What happens to proud people?
5. What do vss. 15–17 teach about Jesus' attitude toward children?

DISCUSSION AND APPLICATION

1. In what circumstances are you like the repentant tax collector? When is your life like the Pharisee's?
2. What advice is contained in this parable for top-level business executives?
3. What admonition is implied regarding the work attitudes of scrub women or garbage collectors?
4. "Everyone in heaven becomes a child all over again according to v. 17."True or false? Why?
5. How do you account for the disciples' attitude toward the children? How do you explain your attitude toward children in busy circumstances similar to vss. 15–17?

ADDITIONAL RESEARCH

1. Luke presents his gospel from a cultural background unique amongst the gospel writers. This background is discernible in the kinds of people whom Luke describes within Christ's ministry. What evidence of this unique background can be found in this passage?
2. What does *justified* in v. 14 mean?
3. How does the kingdom of God differ from the kingdom of heaven?
4. Look up *Pharisee* and *publican* in a Bible dictionary. How do they differ from one another?
5. Do the two incidents in this study have something in common which justifies their being studied as a unit?

STUDY 3: LUKE 18:18–30

BASIC INFORMATION

1. How would you restate v. 18 if you were asking this question today?
2. What had the rich ruler not done?
3. Show that this passage does not close heaven's door to the wealthy. Cite the verse which applies.
4. State in one sentence the central truth which vss. 18–30 teach.
5. What instruction do we gain from the exchange in vss. 28–30?

DISCUSSION AND APPLICATION

1. A famous missionary once said: "He is no fool who forsakes that which he cannot keep, in order to obtain that which he cannot lose." How does that relate to this passage in Luke?
2. What have you left to follow Christ?
3. Who are some famous people today who cling to material wealth rather than live for God? Who are some successful people who are not hindered by this problem?
4. Do you know any morally-sensitive public school teachers who feel that it is fanatical to subject everything to Christ's leadership? Are you acquainted with any taxicab drivers or file clerks who feel the same way?
5. Why was the rich man in this Scripture passage "very sorrowful":
   (a) He resented Jesus' position of authority.
   (b) Material values were the most important thing in his life.

(c) It was theologically impossible for him to be saved.

(d) He couldn't take advice.

6. Does his sorrow indicate that he didn't think Jesus was wise and good?

7. Should we forsake our personal ambitions to gain a reward in heaven?

8. What keeps you from following Christ more closely?

ADDITIONAL RESEARCH

1. Why did the rich ruler call Jesus *Good Master*?

2. Is this the same young man as in Matthew 19:20, 22?

3. What school of thought in educational psychology emphasizes that we are motivated by reward? How does that relate to v. 30?

STUDY 4: LUKE 18:31–43

BASIC INFORMATION

1. To whom did Jesus reveal His coming sufferings?

2. Find the verses in Luke 23 which fulfill each prediction of vss. 32–33.

3. How did Jesus' followers react to this prophecy?

4. What three different names (or titles) were used to describe Christ (vss. 37, 38, 41)?

5. What did the blind man want?

6. How did he respond to Jesus' miracle?

DISCUSSION AND APPLICATION

1. How would you react if you were passing a blind man, begging alongside the road, while you were hurrying toward a busy shopping center to purchase groceries?
2. What needs do you have which Jesus could heal? Is there a deeper need underlying these?
3. Have you ever cried out to Jesus as this blind man did?

ADDITIONAL RESEARCH

1. What is the geographical link between vss. 31–34 and vss. 35–43?
2. Why did the blind man call Jesus the *Son of David*?
3. What new information concerning the true identity of Jesus is reported in this passage?
4. Why did Jesus speak of going *up* to Jerusalem and not *down*?

STUDY 5: LUKE 19:1–10

BASIC INFORMATION

1. Where was Jesus as this story opens?
2. Notice what Zacchaeus did and what happened to him. Suppose that you were talking to a friend over the telephone and describing Zacchaeus. What would you say?
3. What was the crowd's reaction to this incident?
4. Find the verse that summarizes the lesson taught in this passage and then rewrite this lesson in your own words.

DISCUSSION AND APPLICATION

1. "Since Zacchaeus promised to repay four times the amount to the people he had cheated, therefore it is necessary today for people who become Christians to do the same thing." True or false? Why?

2. The principal sin of those who murmured (v. 7) was:
   (a) jealousy
   (b) disbelieving
   (c) gossip
   (d) perverting the law

3. If someone climbed onto the platform where Billy Graham was preaching, how would you feel toward that person? Is that similar or different than Zacchaeus' case?

4. On what grounds could Jesus declare that salvation had come to Zacchaeus' house? Was it something Zacchaeus had done? His faith? The faith of his family?

5. What advice does this passage offer a non-Christian?

ADDITIONAL RESEARCH

1. Look up several outlines of Jesus' life in Bible commentaries, surveys, introductions, or Bibles with supplementary aids. Then fit Luke 18—22 into Jesus' itinerary.

2. What do you know about the phrase *Son of Man*? How does v. 10 help to answer this question?

STUDY 6: LUKE 19:11-27

BASIC INFORMATION

1. Restate each of the incidents in this parable in a sentence or two.
2. Does this passage teach that unfaithfulness to Christ will be punished?
3. What motive for loyalty to Christ is suggested? Give a verse to prove your answer.
4. Describe the thinking of the third servant.
5. The chief failing of the wicked servant was:
   (a) jealousy
   (b) laziness
   (c) selfishness
   (d) covetousness
   (e) a combination of some of these

DISCUSSION AND APPLICATION

1. What abilities or assets do you have which you have not been using for the Lord? Is it fair to compare the *pounds* in this passage with our abilities?
2. What business experience might compare to the situation in this parable?
3. On the basis of this story, what advice would you give a weak Christian?
4. How do you feel toward the nobleman? Do you sometimes have harsh feelings toward God for giving you, in your opinion, a raw deal in life?
5. Does this parable apply more directly to Christians or to non-Christians?

ADDITIONAL RESEARCH

1. Find other parables in which the topic is similar

to this passage and compare or contrast the lesson in each to this parable in vss. 11–27.
2. What are several answers to the charge that v. 27 represents cruelty?
3. How does the percentage of profit in vss. 16–20 compare to interest on investment bonds today?

STUDY 7: LUKE 19:28–40

BASIC INFORMATION

1. Locate the places in v. 29 on a map.
2. How did Jesus obtain the donkey?
3. Explain the actions of these people:
   (a) disciples
   (b) crowd
   (c) Pharisees
4. List all of the means employed to exalt Jesus within this passage.

DISCUSSION AND APPLICATION

1. How does this incident compare or contrast with the parades welcoming home American P.O.W.'s from North Vietnamese prison camps?
2. "The people who praised Jesus were two-faced. They really didn't mean it, but just went along with the mob." Do you agree with this statement?
3. How could you praise God more fully?
4. Was Jesus worthy of the praise in this passage?

ADDITIONAL RESEARCH

1. Why was it important in God's plan for Jesus to enter Jerusalem in this way?
2. What were the social causes for the crowd's demonstration?
3. On what Scriptural basis did the Pharisees order Jesus to rebuke His disciples?
4. Write a dialogue of the disciples' conversation with the owner of the donkey.

STUDY 8: LUKE 19:41–48

BASIC INFORMATION

1. What did Jesus predict regarding Jerusalem?
2. How did Jesus express His feeling for the city?
3. List the features you would include if you were painting the scene portrayed in v. 41.
4. What was Jesus' reaction when He entered the temple?
5. Why didn't the Jewish leaders kill Jesus now?

DISCUSSION AND APPLICATION

1. How do you express your feelings of sorrow? Does it help to know how Jesus felt at this time?
2. What warning to the rebellious is contained in Jesus' lament?
3. "Jesus was guilty of trespassing on others' property when he cleansed the temple." True or false? Why?
4. How would you have reacted to this incident if you had been one of those conducting financial transactions in the temple?

ADDITIONAL RESEARCH

1. Can you identify v. 43 in history? Can you name other cities where this happened?
2. Why did Luke give an editorial opinion in vss. 47–48?
3. What was the legitimate function of moneychangers in the temple?
4. Suppose that you are a reporter for the *Jerusalem Daily News*. You are assigned the temple incident. By the time you arrive on the scene it is all over. You interview several witnesses who were inside the temple when the incident occurred. Write a news article of several paragraphs. Don't forget to select a heading for the article.

STUDY 9: LUKE 20:1–18

BASIC INFORMATION

1. What was Jesus doing in the Temple on this occasion?
2. Explain how the scribes and chief priests undid themselves.
3. How does the story in vss. 9–18 relate to the life of Jesus?
4. How does the mistreatment of the beloved son differ from that experienced by the other messengers?
5. What happened to the evil husbandmen?

DISCUSSION AND APPLICATION

1. By what authority or right do you tell others about the gospel (v. 1)? Do you violate their

rights if you witness to them? Do you violate the rights of a homeowner if you tell him his house is on fire? Or is that a different situation?

2. Do church members sometimes act the same way as the culprits in vss. 10, 11, and 15?

3. Can you think of a political figure who mistreats others to maintain power?

4. Are the kidnappings of government officials similar or different than v. 10?

5. Who possesses authority in school? Home? Business? Church? What is the source of this authority? Do police have the right to search your home? Is it all right for them to bug your telephone? Where does authority begin and end?

6. Choose the proper basis of authority from the following alternatives:
   (a) In the My Lai Massacre Lt. William Calley defended his actions by asserting that he had to obey the orders of his superiors.
   (b) In the Watergate case one of the witnesses, Henry Peterson, asserted that he had to be accountable to himself.
   (c) Martin Luther made his break from Rome on the basis of what he read in the Bible.

ADDITIONAL RESEARCH

1. What was Jesus' authority for His work? John the Baptist's? The prophets'?

2. Explain v. 18.

3. What is *the gospel* (v. 1)?

STUDY 10: LUKE 20:19-26

BASIC INFORMATION

1. How did the scribes compliment Jesus in the introduction to their question?
2. How would you describe Jesus on the basis of this incident?
3. Does Jesus endorse paying taxes to sinful Rome in this passage?
4. Summarize this passage in three sentences or less.

DISCUSSION AND APPLICATION

1. Does Jesus' answer show that He preferred logic or force?
2. What do you dislike most about the scribes and Pharisees? Do they have any virtues?
3. How do people simulate religion today?
4. This passage teaches:
    (a) respect for law and order
    (b) separation of church and state
    (c) salvation by grace
    (d) none of the above
    (e) all of the above
5. How is this passage related to sit-ins and street demonstrations?
6. If it is true that we should give God whatever belongs to Him, then what belongs to Him in your life?

ADDITIONAL RESEARCH

1. List the Pharisees' sins during this confrontation.
2. If you had been doing public relations for the

scribes and Pharisees, how would you have endeavored to improve their public image?

STUDY 11: LUKE 20:27–44

BASIC INFORMATION

1. What was unusual about the woman in this story?
2. Do angels marry?
3. Did Jesus' comments support or oppose the Sadducees' idea of the resurrection?
4. What question did Jesus ask His opponents?

DISCUSSION AND APPLICATION

1. What encouragement does the hope of resurrection give to the people in the following situations:
   (a) bereaved persons
   (b) people with financial problems
   (c) mothers with cranky children
   (d) students with failing grades
2. How could you restate vss. 37–38?
3. Does this passage imply that husbands and wives will have a different relationship in heaven?
4. What aspects of your life are affected most by Jesus' answer in this passage?

ADDITIONAL RESEARCH

1. What were the Jewish laws regarding marriage for widows?

2. What eschatology (last things) do vss. 27–36 teach?

3. Explain Jesus' purpose in vss. 41–44.

4. In the margin of your Bible, mark in red the words Jesus spoke. With a black pencil, mark the words of the scribes and Pharisees. Mark in blue pencil those phrases written by Luke.

STUDY 12: LUKE 20:45—21:4

BASIC INFORMATION

1. Describe the Pharisees' public demeanor.

2. Jesus denounces their long prayers because_____.

3. Does this passage teach how we should contribute to the church?

4. How do vss. 45–47 relate to vss. 1–4?

DISCUSSION AND APPLICATION

1. How are we tempted today to parade our Christianity?

2. Do you know anyone who contributes as much for benevolence as this widow?

3. What is a fair percentage of income for a Christian to give to his church?

4. Does stewardship include more than money? If not, why? If so, give specific examples.

5. The main focus of this passage is on:
   (a) tithing
   (b) pride
   (c) sacrifice

ADDITIONAL RESEARCH

1. What did He mean when Jesus spoke of devouring widows' houses?
2. What other passages in Luke deal with women? Which of these accounts are not in Matthew or Mark?
3. What do I Corinthians 16 and Galatians 6 add to the topic of Christian giving?
4. Describe the procedure for giving to the Jewish treasury. How much were New Testament Jews expected to contribute?

STUDY 13: LUKE 21:5–38

BASIC INFORMATION

1. What circumstances evoked Jesus' comment in v. 6?
2. What are some of the awful things that He predicted?
3. How should believers react to wars according to this passage?
4. What was Jesus' prediction concerning Jerusalem?
5. Choose a heading for these verses.

DISCUSSION AND APPLICATION

1. How can one determine who is a false Christ (v. 8)?
2. Are these predictions coming to pass in our day?
3. Do verses eleven and twenty-five relate to UFO's?

4. Is there cause for alarm in our generation?
5. What comfort for Christians is contained in this chapter?
6. What advice for the unbeliever is contained here?
7. How can we avoid exaggerated interpretations or false scares?

ADDITIONAL RESEARCH

1. To whom do verses fifteen and seventeen apply?
2. What did Jesus mean when He said that heaven and earth would pass away, but His words would not pass away?
3. Research the following topics:
   (a) the pretribulation view of Christ's second coming
   (b) the posttribulation view
   (c) the belief that this passage foretells the fall of Jerusalem in 70 A.D.

REFLECTIONS ON LUKE

1. How many incidents in these chapters show Jesus helping the outcast, the underdog, or the poor?
2. What was Jesus' evaluation of riches according to Luke?
3. Does Luke's attitude toward women differ from that of the other gospel writers?
4. Describe Jesus' character as presented by Luke. What is your reaction to Christ? In what ways does Jesus qualify to influence your life?

5. What new understanding did you gain from Luke toward a more meaningful prayer life?

6. Did you discover a broader understanding of the concept of stewardship?

7. It is sometimes asserted that Luke had a special concern for Gentiles. What evidence can you find in the Scripture passages of these studies to prove or disprove this idea?

3

MATTHEW

The Climax of Jesus' Ministry
Chapters 26—28

STUDY 1: MATTHEW 26:1–16

BASIC INFORMATION

1. How far off was the Passover at the opening of this passage?
2. What did Jesus' plotters want to avoid?
3. On what part of Jesus' body did the woman pour perfume?
4. What was the disciples' reaction to this gesture and what was Jesus' response to them?
5. How did Jesus defend the woman and endorse her action?

DISCUSSION AND APPLICATION

1. "The Jewish leaders felt they were doing the right thing." Do you agree or disagree? Why?
2. Is there plotting against Christian leaders in your church or community?
3. Have you seen an expensive item given to the church when the money paid for the gift should

47

have been used to alleviate suffering? Is this
different than the anointing of Jesus?

4. How do you think Judas rationalized his betrayal?

5. How do Christians rationalize their wrongdoing
today?

ADDITIONAL RESEARCH

1. Find three examples of uproars during Jesus'
ministry.

2. Pretend that you are a trial lawyer defending the
woman's action. What would you say? If you
were the prosecuting attorney?

3. Was the price of betrayal foreshadowed in the
Old Testament?

4. Can you find evidence for also placing Simon
the leper in Christ's earlier ministry?

5. What else had occurred at Bethany during Jesus'
earthly ministry?

STUDY 2: MATTHEW 26:17–35

BASIC INFORMATION

1. In preparation for the Last Supper, Jesus told
His disciples to _____.

2. What four things did Jesus do with the bread?

3. Jesus declared that He would eat with them
again. When would that be?

4. How did Peter react to Jesus' prediction regarding Peter's denial?

DISCUSSION AND APPLICATION

1. Do vss. 17–19 have the atmosphere of Secret Service agents at work?
2. What message do vss. 26–28 have for the non-Christian?
3. Have you experienced or heard recounted the last meal with a soldier before he left for World War II, the Korean War, or Vietnam? Describe the feelings.
4. Why did each of the disciples examine himself as a possible traitor? Does this mirror your own reaction to the fact of Jesus' death? How did the disciples feel toward Judas later, in your opinion?
5. Why is the Lord's Supper called *communion* in I Corinthians 10? What does Communion have to do with fellowship? Could we observe Communion in different ways today to foster awareness of our union with one another?
6. How can you prepare yourself to benefit more from Communion?
7. Do you have any ideas on how Communion might be improved in your church?

ADDITIONAL RESEARCH

1. What were the eating habits in Jesus' day?
2. The other gospels also record this supper. What additional information do they supply?
3. How many instances can you find in the New Testament in which Peter acted impulsively as in v. 33?
4. What does "my blood of the new testament" mean?
5. Does v. 28 teach a substitutionary view of the atonement?

6. What does this passage teach concerning the following questions:
   (a) Do the elements of bread and juice actually become the body and blood of the Lord or does He intend to make them a symbol as He holds them in His hand?
   (b) Do Christians profit by partaking of the elements through the faith they have within?

STUDY 3: MATTHEW 26:36–46

BASIC INFORMATION

1. How many disciples went with Jesus to the Garden of Gethsemane?
2. What was Jesus' posture during these prayers?
3. What was the disciples' posture during Jesus prayers?
4. Jesus pleaded: "_____ and _____ that you enter not into temptation."
5. How many times did Jesus go to pray?

DISCUSSION AND APPLICATION

1. Do you identify with the sleepy disciples? What would it take to get Christians to pray more than they do?
2. How do you think Jesus felt when he found the three disciples sleeping?
3. Do you pray that you will not be tempted?
4. Is it possible for public officials to overcome temptation?
5. Compare and contrast Jesus' prayers in

Gethsemane with Abraham Lincoln's prayers at the time of the American Civil War.

6. How does Jesus' anguish at Gethsemane compare to the following:
   (a) married couples in the process of divorce
   (b) parents whose children go wrong
   (c) an alcoholic who suddenly realizes his condition

7. "I think that Jesus' submission in prayer is beyond the ability of mere men. Therefore I won't try to practice this part of His example." Do you agree or disagree?

ADDITIONAL RESEARCH

1. On what other occasions were Peter, James, and John alone with Jesus?

2. To what cup did Jesus refer in v. 39? Is this related to v. 38 or to II Corinthians 5:21? Can you find another helpful cross-reference?

3. Why did Jesus ask to be released from this cup?

4. What does this passage reveal about Jesus' relationship to His Father?

STUDY 4: MATTHEW 26:47–68

BASIC INFORMATION

1. Tell how Jesus was arrested.

2. What accusation did the two false witnesses bring?

3. What does Jesus openly declare about Himself in v. 64?

4. What verdict did this court produce?

DISCUSSION AND APPLICATION

1. In relation to v. 51, what would you have done if you had been there?
2. How do we betray Jesus today at work, school, recreation, or in the home?
3. How would you react if someone treated you as they did Jesus in vss. 67–68?
4. Can you name some people who are being unjustly condemned?
5. What in this passage might be helpful to explain to someone who is not a committed Christian?
6. What in this passage could motivate Christians to live more like Christ?
7. Choose a heading or title for this passage as if it were an article in the *Jerusalem Times*.

ADDITIONAL RESEARCH

1. How does the disciples' fear (v. 56) substantiate the resurrection of Jesus?
2. Why did Judas choose a kiss as his signal?
3. Did the Jews have grounds in their law to condemn Jesus?
4. Name some other traitors in history. Research their motives. For example, how do Benedict Arnold's motives differ from those of Judas? Does your attitude toward Christ ever involve evil motives?

STUDY 5: MATTHEW 26:69–75

BASIC INFORMATION

1. What locality did the maid associate with Jesus?

2. How did that gathering surmise Peter's home-land?
3. Exactly what did Peter say each time?
4. Name the animal which indicted Peter.
5. Have you ever experienced guilt or sorrow similar to Peter's? How did Peter feel in v. 75?

DISCUSSION AND APPLICATION

1. Children sometimes deny their guilt when con-fronted by their parents. How does this compare to Peter's denial?
2. How do high school students sometimes deny Christ? Athletes? Housewives? Construction workers? Salesmen?
3. What lesson could this denial teach Christians? Non-Christians?
4. Would situation ethics condone Peter's action?
5. What can a repentant man do in addition to sorrowing? That is, can he *do* something? Did Peter make amends later?

ADDITIONAL RESEARCH

1. Is there a difference between deception and lying?
2. Is Peter's denial related to Matthew 10:33? Matthew 16:16–18?

STUDY 6: MATTHEW 27:1–26

BASIC INFORMATION

1. Find three things done by the Jewish leaders in vss. 1–2.

2. When did Judas feel remorse?
3. What people had some influence on Pilate?
4. Summarize each incident in this passage in one sentence.

DISCUSSION AND APPLICATION

1. Can you recall a good example of remorse from literature or history or current events? Does *Macbeth* qualify?
2. Have you ever felt remorse for some act?
3. What do you think caused Judas's admission that Jesus was innocent (v. 4)?
4. If you had been Barabbas, how would you have felt toward the mob? Toward Pilate? Toward Jesus?
5. "If Jesus had defended Himself, He probably would have been released." Do you agree or disagree? Why?
6. How do the dynamics of the mob before Pilate compare to the masses at the Nazi rallies of Hitler? Anti-Vietnam demonstrations? Anti-abortion assemblies?
7. Should Pilate have felt guilty about his decision? Why or why not?

ADDITIONAL RESEARCH

1. Research the reference to Jeremiah in vss. 6–10 by using Bible commentaries.
2. Was Jesus' answer in v. 11 affirmative?
3. In God's sight, did these Jews actually fix their guilt upon their children?
4. What is the logical connection between vss. 1–10 and vss. 11–26?

BASIC INFORMATION

1. What were the soldiers doing when Christ was on the cross? The spectators?
2. What occurred when Jesus "yielded up his spirit"?
3. What was the reaction of the soldiers guarding the cross?
4. Who were the women at the crucifixion and what did they do?
5. How did the Jews seek to counteract Jesus' followers?

DISCUSSION AND APPLICATION

1. Choose the sentence which most nearly matches your response to the description in these verses:
   (a) Oh! It's so gruesome.
   (b) It's too good to be true! Jesus died for me.
   (c) How beautiful are the ugly scars on His body.
   (d) How unworthy I feel.
2. "I'd like to know what it means to be a Christian." What information does this passage provide for such a request?
3. If you had been in the Roman army and were assigned to guard the cross, would you have refused?
4. Without having the scene explained to him, might a bystander have thought that Jesus was just another criminal being executed? Would the crucifixion have been opaque without the interpretation provided in the New Testament writings?
5. Jesus spoke several times while He was suffer-

ing on the cross. Which statement communicates the most to you? Which one causes you to feel what it cost Jesus to die for you?

(a) "I thirst."
(b) "Behold thy son! Behold thy mother!"
(c) "It is finished."
(d) "My God, My God, why hast thou forsaken me?"
(e) Others?

6. What do you think the following persons would have said if they had been the Roman soldier in v. 54:

(a) Joseph Stalin
(b) Bertrand Russell
(c) J. Edgar Hoover
(d) Marilyn Monroe
(e) Nat Turner
(f) William Tyndale

7. What motivated Joseph of Arimathea to go to Pilate?

ADDITIONAL RESEARCH

1. Compare this incident at Golgotha with the summary in I Peter 2:24. The prophecy in Isaiah 53. The doctrines of propitiation, justification, and atonement.

2. Select several hymns which most correctly depict Jesus' passion.

STUDY 8: MATTHEW 28:1–10

BASIC INFORMATION

1. List the people in this incident.
2. Describe the angel.

3. What emotions did the women experience?
4. Can you find three commands given here by Jesus?

DISCUSSION AND APPLICATION

1. If Jesus had not risen from death, how would your life have been different in the past twenty-four hours?
2. What comfort does this story offer someone who fears darkness, high places, highway driving, or death?
3. Do you believe that Jesus died for your sins and rose again to provide eternal life for you personally?
4. Would Abraham have believed Christ's resurrection if it had been foretold to him?
5. What would you have exclaimed to the eleven disciples if Jesus had instructed you to go and tell the disciples?
6. What does the rock opera, *Jesus Christ Superstar*, do with the resurrection of Christ? What is your reaction to this?
7. What would you recommend as appropriate television programs at Easter?

ADDITIONAL RESEARCH

1. Find some of Jesus' predictions of His resurrection.
2. How does I Corinthians 15:35–44 amplify v. 9? How are I Corinthians 15:55 and v. 5 related?
3. Name three great leaders who were martyred and whose followers later claimed to see them and touch them.

STUDY 9: MATTHEW 28:11–20

BASIC INFORMATION

1. Retell in your own words the conversation between the guards and the Jewish leaders mentioned in this passage.
2. What results did the guards' story bring?
3. To what place did the eleven journey?
4. What instructions did Jesus give them?
5. What instructions did Jesus give for those who are baptized?

DISCUSSION AND APPLICATION

1. What difference can this Great Commission make in your kitchen if you take it more seriously than you have in the past?
2. List several ways that Christians could witness more to the unbelieving world.
3. If one is to be a Christian, is it necessary that he or she observe what Jesus commanded?
4. "Since Jesus taught His disciples to teach the new converts everything that He had commanded, this means that all of us are to obey all of the commands given to the disciples." True or false? Why? Does this prove that everyone should be baptized?
5. How does the Christian's hope of resurrection relate to Jesus' words in this passage?

ADDITIONAL RESEARCH

1. Ask two people what heading they would give to this passage.
2. Can you find a Scripture reference other than a verse in the four gospels where the Great Commission is given in essence?

3. Write down several questions which you have after reading this passage and then find answers to them.

REFLECTIONS ON MATTHEW

1. If you had known nothing about Jesus, what would your concept of Him be after reading Matthew's portrayal in these chapters?

2. What is the significance of Christ's death, in your opinion? What did it accomplish? Toward whom was it directed?

3. Give several examples of Matthew's use of the Old Testament. What was his purpose in alluding to these passages? Was it different than the aim of other gospel writers?

4. Suppose that you are visiting with someone who claims that the stories about Jesus' resurrection were a hoax. Would the following question be a meaningful rebuttal? "Why were not the Jews, who were eyewitnesses of these events, more effective in refuting these stories?"

5. The following statements refer to the uniqueness of Matthew's presentation of Jesus. Are any of them illustrated in chapters twenty-six through twenty-eight?
    (a) Jesus is portrayed as the King of the Jews and the Son of David.
    (b) The *kingdom* refers to an earthly reign titled "the Kingdom of Heaven."
    (c) Several long discourses or addresses are unique to Matthew.
    (d) There is an unusual emphasis on the word *church* not found in the other gospels.

4

ACTS

Chapters 1—4, 13—15

STUDY 1: ACTS 1

BASIC INFORMATION

1. To whom did Luke write?
2. Why did Luke write?
3. How did the Christians spend their time between the ascension and Pentecost?
4. What happened to Jesus after He spoke at the Mount of Olives?
5. How did they select a twelfth disciple?

DISCUSSION AND APPLICATION

1. Try to recall your words, written to a friend or acquaintance, concerning what you knew and believed about Jesus.
2. What aspects would you stress if you were to paint the scene of the ascension? Could you depict it in abstract symbols?
3. C. S. Lewis once explained that the uniqueness of a miracle did not disturb him because there is

at least one unique phenomena which is definitely true—the existence of the universe. Does this idea apply to the ascension?
4. Should we pray more earnestly before annual church elections? Would it make a difference?
5. How do you suppose Matthias felt when "the lot fell" (v. 26)? Joseph Justus? How do you feel immediately after being elected to a position of responsibility? How do you feel when you have been passed over for a position of responsibility?

ADDITIONAL RESEARCH

1. How is casting lots in this situation different than gambling?
2. Is there a correlation between apparent contradictions in the New Testament accounts of Judas's suicide?
3. Find Scripture references which reveal how the ascension of Jesus affects our prayer lives today. Are you conscious of this as you pray?

STUDY 2: ACTS 2:1–13

BASIC INFORMATION

1. Describe what the people in v. 1 saw and heard.
2. What attracted the attention of people outside this gathering place?
3. What was the effect of the outpouring of the Holy Spirit?
4. Why were the multitude amazed?
5. The skeptical explanation for this strange event was that_____.

DISCUSSION AND APPLICATION

1. Some have described Pentecost as the birth of the church. Do you agree?
2. Have you ever witnessed or experienced tongues? What is your evaluation of this phenomenon?
3. Recall notable Christian events you have attended such as a revival, church dedication, denominational rally, or evangelistic services. Compare your emotions and impressions then with those of the Christians on Pentecost.
4. How do outsiders belittle Christianity today?

ADDITIONAL RESEARCH

1. What was the Jewish day of Pentecost?
2. Find other Scripture references to being "filled with the Holy Spirit."
3. Plot on a map the countries noted in vss. 9–12.
4. Is the speaking in languages in this passage the same or different from that found in I Corinthians 12 and 14?

STUDY 3: ACTS 2:14–47

BASIC INFORMATION

1. What two defenses did Peter use to refute the accusation of drunkenness?
2. What did men do to Jesus while He was on earth, according to vss. 22–24? On the other hand, what did Jesus Himself do according to these verses?
3. Where is Jesus now?

4. Where is David now?
5. What prescription did Peter recommend to his listeners (v. 38)?
6. If the hearers would do what Peter suggested, they would receive_____.
7. What were the results of this sermon?

DISCUSSION AND APPLICATION

1. On many other occasions the Jews became angry when they heard the confession in v. 36. What explains their reaction in this case?
2. Can you recall a distinct experience of the Holy Spirit at work in your life? How could you discover more about what He wants to do in and through you?
3. How could your church profit from the example of the early church?
4. "I think we should have smaller Bible study groups who meet in the homes. Then we could cultivate the closeness that the early Christians experienced." Do you agree or disagree? Why?
5. How is the church's activity in v. 45 different from Marxist communism?

ADDITIONAL RESEARCH

1. Did the prophet Joel accurately predict what happened at Pentecost?
2. Is "receive the Holy Spirit" (v. 38) identical to "filled with the Holy Spirit" (2:4)?
3. What role does the Holy Spirit perform in the sanctification of the believer?
4. Cite examples from Jesus' ministry to support Peter's declaration in v. 22.
5. Is the *prophesy* in v. 17 the same as the reference in I Corinthians 12 and 14?

STUDY 4: ACTS 3

BASIC INFORMATION

1. Where did Peter and John go?
2. In modern society, what time of day is the ninth hour (v. 1)?
3. People would carry a certain lame man and lay him_____.
4. When Peter spoke to the cripple in the name of Jesus, the text notes that parts of the man's body were affected. Which parts?
5. How did Peter make the transition from healing to preaching Jesus?
6. Restate v. 19 in your own words.
7. To whom was Jesus first sent?

DISCUSSION AND APPLICATION

1. Are there people today who expect that becoming a Christian will insure material blessings? Do the circumstances of Peter in v. 6 relate to this expectation?
2. The lame man asked for alms and received healing. Can you recall a similar result in your prayer life?
3. The lame man's reaction was a witness to the observers (vss. 8–11). How could the Christian's expressions of joy be a witness to the people about us?
4. Should we expect to see people healed today?

ADDITIONAL RESEARCH

1. Can you find Old Testament predictions of a suffering Messiah which Jesus fulfilled?
2. How does the outline of this sermon compare to

that of the sermon in Acts 2? Is it basically the same or different?

3. Research the controversy which has resulted from differing interpretations of v. 21.
4. What light do vss. 25–26 shed on the role of Israel in God's plan of salvation?

STUDY 5: ACTS 4

BASIC INFORMATION

1. Who were upset with Peter and John? Why?
2. What question did they ask Peter and John?
3. Whose observation is presented in v. 13?
4. What was the dilemma confronting the religious leaders in vss. 14–17?
5. How did Peter and John react to the religious leaders?
6. Can you divide the prayer in vss. 24–30 into two main parts?
7. List three facts from vss. 31–37 which reveal the fellowship of the early church in Jerusalem.

DISCUSSION AND APPLICATION

1. Does v. 12 disallow the possibility that the religions of Mohammed and Buddha include some truth? How does John 14:6 compare to this verse? Does this challenge you to respond to Christ or not? Why?
2. "We don't want to hear another peep out of you regarding Jesus of Nazareth coming back to life." Is that a fair restatement of v. 18? If not, how would you restate it?

3. Did this admonition in v. 18 silence Peter and John? Compare this scene with the description of the disciples in John 20:19.
4. Do you know of any Christians today who practice some or all of the virtues in v. 32?
5. Should churches become involved in welfare work (v. 34)?

ADDITIONAL RESEARCH

1. Were there 5000 additional people who believed (v. 4) or were these 5000 included in the 3000 who became Christians at Pentecost?
2. Find the sentences in this chapter which are clearly the words of the writer of Acts.
3. Is "filled with the Holy Spirit" in v. 31 the same kind of experience as in 2:4?

STUDY 6: ACTS 13:1–12

BASIC INFORMATION

1. What roles did Barnabas, Simeon Niger, Lucius of Cyrene, and Manaen have in the church at Antioch?
2. What were the circumstances when this church received the message from the Holy Spirit?
3. Describe the farewell service for Barnabas and Saul.
4. Who summoned the missionaries? What position did he hold?
5. Which of the following characteristics did Saul

exhibit when he was filled with the Holy Spirit here:

(a) timidity
(b) boldness in rebuking evil
(c) winning souls

DISCUSSION AND APPLICATION

1. Was Paul wrong to label the magician as he did in v. 10?
2. Imagine that you are the magician. Describe your feelings toward Paul. In your disputes, is it helpful to identify with your opponents' feelings?
3. Compare the magicians of today with Barjesus.
4. "Our churches today should fast and pray as in v. 3." Do you agree with this opinion?
5. How can we experience more of the Holy Spirit's leading, as described in verses two and four?
6. Should the church today recruit missionaries?

ADDITIONAL RESEARCH

1. Is v. 3 an example of ordination?
2. Find out all that you can about Sergius Paulus. Imagine that he is an acquaintance of yours, and compose an introduction of several sentences for an audience waiting to hear him lecture.
3. If you had been there, what evidence could you offer to support Luke's statement that Paul was "filled with the Holy Spirit" (v. 9)?
4. Would it be accurate to say that Paul placed a curse on a man who had made a contract with the devil (vss. 9–11)?
5. Which missionary journey of Paul do chapters

thirteen and fourteen describe? Using a map, trace Paul's route on this journey.

STUDY 7: ACTS 13:13–52

BASIC INFORMATION

1. To whom did Paul preach at Antioch of Pisidia?
2. How did Paul gain their attention?
3. List the Old Testament persons whom Paul mentions.
4. What kind of Gentiles were in the synagogue of the Jews?
5. What event in the life of Jesus did Paul emphasize?
6. Paul gave a promise and a warning in vss. 39–41. What are they?
7. What were the results of Paul's sermons in Antioch?

DISCUSSION AND APPLICATION

1. Paul witnessed in the synagogue and people listened. Where could you witness?
2. Has anyone ever inquired about your religious beliefs?
3. Has your witness for Christ ever been opposed?
4. How should the church respond when someone arrives teaching new ideas? What should the church do if a group walked in during a worship services displaying placards regarding abortion?

ADDITIONAL RESEARCH

1. What is the name of the modern country where this incident took place?
2. *The Word* is mentioned in vss. 44, 46, 48, and 49 (also 13:5, 7, and 26). What do these verses reveal about Paul's attitude toward the Word of God? In a concordance, find other verses in Acts which use this phrase.
3. Who were the *religious proselytes* who followed Paul and Barnabas?
4. How is *forgiveness* (v. 38) related to *justified* (v. 39)?
5. Many events of the Old Testament are referred to here, providing a partial outline of the history of the Old Testament. What other key events or eras would you add to make this outline more complete?

STUDY 8: ACTS 14

BASIC INFORMATION

1. What cities did Paul and Barnabas visit in this chapter?
2. Why did the audience in Lystra worship Paul and Barnabas?
3. How did Barnabas and Paul use this situation to witness for Christ?
4. How did they encourage the believers on their return to these cities?
5. What did they do when they returned to Antioch in Syria?

DISCUSSION AND APPLICATION

1. Paul and Barnabas fled in verses six and twenty. Does that prove they were cowards?
2. Why didn't Paul organize a group of militants to wage guerilla warfare against the agitating Jews?
3. In relation to vss. 14–15, do people sometimes give you more credit than you deserve? Why is that difficult to handle? How can you use this as an opportunity to witness, as Paul did?
4. Why do we place some people on a pedestal?
5. How can we encourage new Christians like those in v. 22? What if they were in your present church?
6. Was Paul using sound administrative methods in v. 22?

ADDITIONAL RESEARCH

1. Where does Paul refer to this stoning in his epistles?
2. How does v. 17 relate to the doctrine of common grace?
3. What does v. 23 reveal about ordination? Fasting?
4. Explain the words "gave testimony unto the word of his grace" (v. 3).

STUDY 9: ACTS 15:1–29

BASIC INFORMATION

1. What was creating a controversy in the church at Antioch?

2. What group was causing this controversy?
3. What did the church do?
4. What counsel did Peter offer?
5. What was the result of the deliberation of the church in Jerusalem?

DISCUSSION AND APPLICATION

1. Was racial prejudice the root problem in this controversy?
2. What conduct do established Christians today expect of newer believers that they do not maintain themselves (cf. v. 10)?
3. Suppose that a controversy arises within your church over the issue of continuing to hold evening services. What suggestions would you offer toward a solution?
4. How might you reword and explain v. 11?
5. If you were a Jew and a voting member of this Jerusalem Council, how would you have reacted to the final decision:
   (a) you would have agreed
   (b) you would have opposed the decision
   (c) you wouldn't have had a definite opinion
6. "I think this illustrates a problem which we face today—the church has too many people who emphasize the negative aspect of duty." Do you agree with this opinion?
7. How would the history of the early church have changed if it had decided to adopt the practice in v. 1? Would Christianity have merged into Judaism?

ADDITIONAL RESEARCH

1. Find other disputes which troubled the early church. How were they resolved?

2. Why did the Antioch Christians, seeking direction, send representatives to Jerusalem? Was the advice from the Jerusalem Council to the church in Antioch binding?
3. Is v. 2 a legalistic imposition on the Gentiles at Antioch?
4. Why was the eating of *things strangled* forbidden?

STUDY 10: ACTS 15:30–41

BASIC INFORMATION

1. How did the Antioch Christians react to the message from Jerusalem?
2. What occupied Judas and Silas at Antioch?
3. What was the irritation between Paul and Barnabas?
4. What was the reason for Paul's feelings about John Mark?
5. What happened because of this problem?

DISCUSSION AND APPLICATION

1. Regarding v. 35, how can you teach others about Christ where you are?
2. Does v. 36 relate to follow-up work with new Christians?
3. Does the difference of opinion between Paul and Barnabas indicate that they were not filled with the Spirit at that moment?
4. Does this irritation furnish any lessons for resolving disagreements today?

5. How can we be honest *and* loving when someone contests our principles?
6. Do you think Paul was overreacting to John Mark?

ADDITIONAL RESEARCH

1. What do vss. 30, 33 manifest about the fellowship of churches? Does this chapter begin denominational administration?
2. What does it mean that Judas and Silas were *prophets*?
3. What does history reveal about the missionary work of Barnabas and John Mark on Cyprus?

REFLECTIONS ON ACTS

1. Trace the development of the outreach ministry of the early church by selecting the major incident in each of the past ten studies.
2. Is there a typical outline which is used in most of the sermons in these study passages? Do these sermons show how repentance is related to faith? Are certain steps suggested as a way of salvation?
3. How important is the Holy Spirit in these studies? Would it be more correct to title this book "The Acts of the Holy Spirit" rather than "The Acts of the Apostles"? Reread the verses in the New Testament containing the words "filled with the Spirit" and list the results in each instance. How can we experience this?
4. What distinctive behavior characterized the

early church which we should practice more in our time? How could your church achieve this?

5. If the early church fabricated the stories of what Jesus did, then who would have caused the growth of the early church? Is this dilemma a ground for the reliability of the New Testament?

6. What changed the early followers of Jesus from frightened men hiding behind locked doors (John 20:19) into fearless witnesses (Acts 4 and 13)? Does the resurrection of Jesus speak to this question?

7. What evidence do we have that Luke is the author of the book of Acts? What does the word *we* in various passages prove regarding the author's presence at some of these events?

8. Correlate one incident of your choice in Acts to reference verses in the epistles and show how they explain each other.

5

ROMANS

Chapters 1—6

STUDY 1: ROMANS 1

BASIC INFORMATION

1. What complementary aspects of Christ's nature does Paul note in vss. 3–4?
2. In what way is Paul a *debtor*?
3. How is God characterized in v. 7?
4. Paul thanks God for the Roman Christians' _____.
5. What does the gospel accomplish (v. 16)?
6. Find two attributes of God in vss. 17–18.
7. "Creation testifies to the power of God." True or false?
8. How have men treated this testimony?
9. What does v. 25 reveal about the heart of man?
10. Can you find a synonym for all of the sins listed in vss. 26–32?

DISCUSSION AND APPLICATION

1. How have you been called by Jesus (v. 6)? What does He want you to do?

2. Do the churches of your community view themselves as debtors to the poor, handicapped, divorced, lonely, disturbed, and the delinquent living around them?

3. How many attributes of God can you find in this chapter? Which of these attributes summon personal experiences in your relationship to God?

4. Does nature prove the existence of God? How do I Corinthians 1:27 and 2:10–14 relate to this question?

5. "The evil of men in Romans 1 is evidence that man is born a sinner." Do you agree or disagree? Why?

6. Do you know people today who take pleasure in sin?

ADDITIONAL RESEARCH

1. Which of the following attributes of God are substantiated in this chapter:
   (a) omnipresence
   (b) immutability
   (c) justice
   (d) veracity
   (e) benevolence

2. What is the difference between God's righteousness and His holiness?

3. What is the link between v. 17 and the Protestant Reformation?

4. Explain the Biblical view of homosexuality.

5. What is a *reprobate mind* (v. 28)?

STUDY 2: ROMANS 2

BASIC INFORMATION

1. Why are men inexcusable?
2. What does this passage reveal about the judgment of God?
3. What does this chapter present as the basis for God's judgment of individuals?
4. Contrast God's dealings with good and evil people (vss. 7–10).
5. Are Gentiles exempt from punishment if they have never heard God's law?
6. Why is the disobedience of the Jews so serious according to this passage?
7. Who is a true Jew?

DISCUSSION AND APPLICATION

1. What excuses have you heard men give to justify their evil acts?
2. Psychologists speak of defense mechanisms such as compensation and projection. Do we use these mechanisms when we should be repenting of our sin? If so, recall a distinct example of this from your own life.
3. How would you convince a skeptic that he is a sinner before God?
4. Do you know anyone who is afraid of God's judgment? Does the day of judgment unsettle you?
5. What is ironic about failing to practice what we preach (v. 1)?

ADDITIONAL RESEARCH

1. What two grounds for the eternal condemnation of the heathen are given in Romans 1 and 2?

2. How have the promises to the Jews in the Old Testament been expanded? Are they now fulfilled in the experience of the church?
3. When was circumcision performed in Jewish ritual? What did it signify?
4. Trace Paul's logic in this passage by choosing key phrases which you think advance his explanation.

STUDY 3: ROMANS 3:1–20

BASIC INFORMATION

1. What advantage is there in being a Jew?
2. "Some say that man's sin serves to reveal the justice of God." True or false?
3. How many people are righteous?
4. Are the Jews more righteous than the Gentiles?
5. List the parts of the body which are described in this passage.
6. What is the purpose of the law?

DISCUSSION AND APPLICATION

1. Have you ever wished that you were a Jew? Or wished that you weren't?
2. How does this passage answer non-Christians who question God's justice?
3. How has Paul proved that all men are sinners?
4. Do vss. 10–18 describe your attitude and conduct before you were saved?
5. "After a person becomes a Christian he is never guilty of the shortcomings in vss. 10–18." True or false? Why?

ADDITIONAL RESEARCH

1. What is sin according to the Bible?
2. Can you find other Biblical references to the sins listed in vss. 10–18?
3. Does this passage imply that all people inherit a sinful nature?Do any other Scripture references prove this?

STUDY 4: ROMANS 3:20—4:25

BASIC INFORMATION

1. What did the shedding of Jesus' blood accomplish?
2. Can Abraham boast according to Paul?
3. What do vss. 4–5 reveal about the nature of grace?
4. What historical fact does Paul cite to clinch his argument for the doctrine of salvation by grace?
5. What does v. 17 say?

DISCUSSION AND APPLICATION

1. Does this passage seem too abstract or too profound? If so, what don't you understand?
2. Some people feel that they are good enough and do not need to concern themselves with God's provision for salvation. What does this passage say to this idea?
3. Do you experience remorse for wrongdoing, but also struggle with lingering guilt feelings?
4. Does v. 17 mean that the origin of God's plan for the Gentiles is in the Old Testament?

ADDITIONAL RESEARCH

1. Does v. 26 provide evidence for a penal concept of atonement?
2. Define *redemption*, *propitiation*, and *justification*.
3. How could circumcision be the seal of righteousness (v. 11)?
4. How should we understand Paul's associations of Jesus' death with our sin and Jesus' resurrection with our justification (v. 25)?

STUDY 5: ROMANS 5

BASIC INFORMATION

1. What is the relationship between God and man in v. 1?
2. Rephrase the results of the tribulations in v. 4 with synonyms or summary phrases.
3. When did God commend his love toward men?
4. What sentence passed on all men as a result of one man's disobedience?
5. During the time between Adam and Moses, _____ reigned.
6. What is God's free gift?
7. What was the purpose of the law?
8. What is the relationship between sin and grace in v. 20?

DISCUSSION AND APPLICATION

1. Can you recall a personal experience which illustrates the development from patience to hope as in v. 4?

2. Can you recall experiencing awe at God's love for you?
3. Have you ever felt condemned before God?
4. Could you explain to someone else how God acted in history on your behalf?
5. Right now, are you experiencing God's grace active in your life or is the power of sin stronger?
6. If God's grace increases with the increase of sin, isn't it logical that we should sin more so that grace may increase?

ADDITIONAL RESEARCH

1. How are we saved by Christ's life (v. 10)?
2. Explain *justification* in the context of studies four and five.
3. What do vss. 12–21 teach with regard to the doctrine of the transmission of sin (cf. realistic mode, creationist view, et al).

STUDY 6: ROMANS 6

BASIC INFORMATION

1. According to this chapter shall we continue in sin so that grace may abound?
2. We are_____with Christ by baptism into death.
3. If we have been united with Christ into death, we shall also_____.
4. Having experienced these things, what is the believer's relationship to sin?
5. What is commanded in vss. 11–13?
6. What is the fruit of sin (vss. 21–23)? Of righteousness?

DISCUSSION AND APPLICATION

1. Have you been baptized? If so, why:
   (a) to conform to tradition or societal pressure
   (b) to guarantee salvation
   (c) to obey a command in the Bible

2. If you have not been baptized, how do you respond to Paul's explanation that "we have been planted together in the likeness of his death" and "we shall be also in the likeness of his resurrection"?

3. If you have been baptized as an adult, what can you remember most vividly about the events before, during, and after baptism?

4. Is baptism primarily a symbol, or is it more than this?

5. How can a person be dead and still alive? How is this related to the sanctification of believers?

6. If sin has no more dominion or authority over Christians (v. 14), how does that affect:
   (a) How you carry out your supervisor's orders on the job.
   (b) How you cooperate in the program of your church by attending services, praying for other members, forgiving evil deeds, giving your money, and serving in offices.
   (c) How you act toward other members of your family. Do they feel happy when you are present or uneasy?

7. Whose servant are you (v. 16)?

8. Do you fear the fruit of sin?

ADDITIONAL RESEARCH

1. Does this passage relate to the mode of baptism? If so, how?

2. If Christians have died to sin (v. 7), how is it yet possible for them to sin?

3. How is Romans 6 related to Romans 7 and 8?

REFLECTIONS ON ROMANS

1. Review each study and then choose a heading for each.
2. Who, when, and what was the occasion for writing the book of Romans?
3. These chapters emphasize doctrine, but what practical effects has this study had on your life?
4. Write a brief essay on the topic of the nature of God as presented in the book of Romans. Do the same on the topic of the nature of man.
5. Use the following verses and chapters to outline the process of man finding peace with God: Romans 3:23; 6:23; 5:8; 10:9, 10, 13. How do they represent a step-by-step process describing why men need salvation, how it is provided, and what man's response must be?
6. How do the later chapters in Romans relate to the first six? Can you find three major divisions for this book?
7. Return to the introduction to these studies. Evaluate how you or your group are fulfilling the objectives presented there. Are there some adjustments you could make which are not mentioned there? How could you become more serious and systematic in your Bible study?

6

COLOSSIANS

Chapters 1—4

STUDY 1: COLOSSIANS 1:1–12

BASIC INFORMATION

1. For how many things does Paul thank God? List five things for which gratitude is expressed.
2. What are some results of preaching the gospel according to this passage?
3. Explain the words *being fruitful* (v. 10).
4. What did Epaphras tell Paul about the Colossians?

DISCUSSION AND APPLICATION

1. Does v. 9 mean that Paul prayed for the Colossians at least once every waking moment? If not, what did Paul mean? What instruction does this provide for your own prayer life?
2. Paul gave thanks for specific things. How many items can you list for which you have given God thanks in the last three days? How can we remember to talk to God about the things that

we think about and tell others about—both our joys and problems?

3. Is it possible that Christians who pray regularly might not always possess patience and longsuffering (v. 11)?

4. Recall the circumstances when God gave you special strength to face a particular situation. What feelings did you have before you prayed? After He answered?

5. What kind of a life would be worthy and pleasing to God? Give an example from home, school, church, or country.

ADDITIONAL RESEARCH

1. Find several other New Testament passages that have an impact similar to v. 11.

2. How is the grace of God (v. 6) different from His mercy?

3. Use this passage (especially v. 11) to outline what you could say to another Christian who is experiencing stress. Are you tempted to make your solution too easy and idealistic?

4. How do vss. 1–4 differ from Ephesians 1:1–3?

STUDY 2: COLOSSIANS 1:13–23

BASIC INFORMATION

1. Who has delivered us from the power of darkness?

2. List five things which Jesus did for us according to vss. 13–14 and vss. 21–22.

3. Imagine that you are explaining v. 23 to a new

Christian. Restate this verse in one or two sentences of your own.
4. Can you explain these phrases:
   (a) "image of the invisible God" (v. 15)
   (b) "thrones, or dominions, or principalities, or powers" (v. 16)
5. Of what body is Jesus the head?
6. Who has been reconciled?

DISCUSSION AND APPLICATION

1. If Jesus created all things (v. 16), what bearing does this have on a non-Christian who is not sensitive to spiritual things?
2. If Jesus is the head of the church, how does that affect issues where there are honest differences of opinion such as using pledge cards for the offering, which version of the Bible to use, singing new kinds of music, and the length of ladies' skirts.
3. If Jesus is the head of the church, how does that influence our attitudes toward one another? Do we ever repent of the sins of pride and judging one another?
4. Were you an enemy of God before you turned to Christ (cf. v. 21)? How were you reconciled when you became a Christian?
5. Do you know anyone who is unblameable or unreprovable before God (v. 22)?
6. How could reconciliation as presented in this passage affect two friends who are disagreeing?

ADDITIONAL RESEARCH

1. How does v. 19 relate to the doctrine of the Trinity?

2. Which of the following are descriptions of Jesus based on vss. 15–19:
   (a) eternally begotten
   (b) Creator
   (c) Lamb of God
   (d) Lord of the universe
3. Ask the opinion of a Christian physicist or science teacher regarding the meaning of the word *consist* in v. 17.
4. What is the difference between "first born of every creature" (v. 15) and "first born from the dead" (v. 18)?
5. Does v. 20 suggest that a penalty was paid for our sins?
6. Which of the following can be identified with the "kingdom of his dear Son":
   (a) millenium
   (b) eternal heaven
   (c) church
   (d) God's rule in our hearts

STUDY 3: COLOSSIANS 1:24–29

BASIC INFORMATION

1. What has Paul been doing on behalf of the church?
2. What is the sacred mystery hidden for the ages and revealed only in Christ's coming to earth (vss. 26–27)? Cf. Ephesians 3:3–6.
3. Check the phrase "Christ in you, the hope of glory." Which of these explanations is best:

(a) The Holy Spirit indwells believers.

(b) Even Gentiles can be saved.

(c) Christians should be mature.

4. What were some of the specific things that Paul warned and taught the Colossians to do early in this chapter?

DISCUSSION AND APPLICATION

1. Why was Paul glad that he could suffer (v. 24)? What purpose have your sufferings fulfilled?

2. Has God sent you also to tell about His plan (v. 25)? If so, what are some ways in which you can make this known in your neighborhood? If not, why do you feel excluded from this task?

3. What are some things that unbelievers should be warned about today according to this passage?

4. Is Paul proposing that fear should be used to motivate people toward God (v. 28)? Is fear of punishment a proper motive to influence children to obey parents or criminals to obey the law?

5. Name some things that you think Christians should be warned about.

6. In what areas could you try harder to serve Christ?

ADDITIONAL RESEARCH

1. In what way could Paul fulfill the suffering of Christ for the church (v. 24)?

2. Is there any reason to include the last phrase of v. 23, "whereof I Paul am made a minister," in this study?

3. How is "Christ in you, the hope of glory" related to Ephesians 3:16–17?

4. What new insight does Paul provide regarding the church?

STUDY 4: COLOSSIANS 2:1–10

BASIC INFORMATION

1. Reread the verses where these phrases are found:
   (a) "So walk ye in him"
   (b) "Rooted and built up in him"
   (c) "In whom are hid all the treasures of wisdom and knowledge"
2. Explain the phrase "established in the faith" (v. 7).
3. Match the items in the column on the left with the phrases in the column on the right:

Colossians	tradition of men
rudiments of the world	fulness of Godhead
Christ	absent in the flesh
Paul	received Christ

DISCUSSION AND APPLICATION

1. Do you ever have concern for others as Paul did in v. 1?
2. How can love comfort someone who is afflicted (v. 2)?
3. Explain v. 6 by constructing a brief explanation of receiving Christ which you might share with an airline passenger seated beside you.
4. How does the hymn "Have Thine Own Way, Lord" fit v. 7?
5. How can a housewife, student, or businessman

use their afternoons to walk as in v. 6? In what different ways might they use their mornings as they walk in Christ?

ADDITIONAL RESEARCH

1. What is the significance of the phrase *in Christ* (v. 5) or *in him* (vss. 6–7)? Consult these references as well: Colossians 1:28; 2:20; 3:1, 4; Ephesians 1:3, 11; 2:6, 10, 13, 22; and Romans 6:3, 4, 8, 11.
2. How does v. 9 relate to the concept of the Trinity?
3. What specific philosophy does Paul have in mind in v. 8?

STUDY 5: COLOSSIANS 2:11–15

BASIC INFORMATION

1. Jot down several questions which you have after reading this passage.
2. What is the point when Paul notes the "circumcision made without hands" (v. 11) or "Buried with him in baptism" (v. 12)?
3. Does "being dead in your sins" refer to the same thing as "Buried with him in baptism"?
4. Jesus made an open show of his victory over _____.

DISCUSSION AND APPLICATION

1. If the Christian is circumcised from the sins of the flesh (v. 11), how will this affect the way he

lives after he is saved? How did it change John Newton (the slave trader), Saint Augustine, and Billy Sunday? Do you know of someone else?

2. In v. 13 it speaks of "having forgiven you all trespasses." Describe how you felt when you realized that God had forgiven a specific, sinful action or attitude. Or how do you think you would feel if you had experienced this?

3. In v. 14 it speaks of blotting out Jewish ordinances. What are church traditions today which some people treat as Biblical commands?

4. "Christianity is not basically a matter of do's and don'ts." True or false? Why?

ADDITIONAL RESEARCH

1. Compare v. 12 to Romans 6:1–6. Explain how they deal with the same idea.

2. If Jesus had not literally risen from the dead, how would that affect the meaning of v. 12?

3. In v. 14, what prepares us for v. 15?

4. Does v. 14 mean that the laws of God were destroyed?

5. Relate v. 15 to Ephesians 6:12 and Romans 8:38. On the other hand, compare v. 15 to II Corinthians 2:14.

STUDY 6: COLOSSIANS 2:16–23

BASIC INFORMATION

1. What do these terms refer to: *holyday, new moon, the sabbath days*?

2. Explain who or what is foreshadowed by the references in vss. 16–17. Cf. Hebrews 8:5 and 10:1.

3. What do vss. 21–23 tell about the body?

4. Select a heading for this passage.

DISCUSSION AND APPLICATION

1. John sold his car to someone for a price above its market value. A fellow church member, Bill, complained to some of his friends about John's "dishonesty." Did Bill sin by judging his brother? What does v. 16 offer in this connection?

2. Can you recall an instance when you judged someone in regard to food, Sunday observance, grades in school, or recreational activities?

3. If you had a vision telling you to do something, would you do it even if your conscience bothered you (cf. v. 18)?

4. Why do people follow rules even though they have died with Christ?

5. What are some false relgions we must beware of today?

6. What instruction does v. 17 give to a new Christian trying to decide what amusements or recreation are proper for a follower of Christ? What other passages in the New Testament provide moral guidelines?

ADDITIONAL RESEARCH

1. Relate v. 19 to other verses in Colossians which speak of the Christian being *in him* or *in union with Christ*.

2. What does it mean to be *dead with Christ* (v. 20)? How does this affect one's conduct?

3. Look up the word *Gnosticism* in an encyclopedia

or other reference work. List some of the basic teachings of this philosophy. How is it related to the book of Colossians?

STUDY 7: COLOSSIANS 3:1–11

BASIC INFORMATION

1. What are some examples of the "things which are above" which Christians should pursue?
2. List the things that a person dead and risen with Christ won't do.
3. What is covetousness (v. 5)? How can it be idolatry?
4. Who are the objects of God's wrath? Why does this wrath exist?
5. Why don't Christians lie to one another? Is it because of laws and regulations or is there another reason?

DISCUSSION AND APPLICATION

1. "After reading v. 5 I have come to the conviction that this verse disqualifies most secular magazines and movies from use by Christians." Do you agree or disagree? Why?
2. What changes would take place in churches if v. 2 were taken seriously? How would it affect the recruiting of Sunday school teachers?
3. Do you know of someone whose life changed dramatically after becoming a Christian (cf. v. 7)?
4. What advice would you give a new Christian based on this passage?
5. Does v. 11 support racial integration?

6. If you were involved in a business transaction and your supervisor ordered you to lie about something, how could you handle that situation (v. 9)? What if your job were at stake?

ADDITIONAL RESEARCH

1. How can earthly Christians also be risen with Christ at the right hand of God (v. 1)?
2. What is *evil concupiscence* (v. 5)? How would situation ethics react to this prohibition?
3. Compare v. 5 to Romans 8:13.
4. Find another reference to the wrath of God in the New Testament.
5. Who were the Scythians?

STUDY 8: COLOSSIANS 3:12–17

BASIC INFORMATION

1. What is a basic reason for forgiving people who wrong us (vss. 12–14)?
2. Choose the words that don't fit the pattern of the others:
   (a) kindness
   (b) longsuffering
   (c) quarrel
   (d) peace
   (e) malice
   (f) forgiving
3. What is the responsibility of members of Christ's body according to v. 15?
4. What function does music serve in the Christian experience?
5. What counsel does v. 17 provide as we decide

whether we should or should not do something?

DISCUSSION AND APPLICATION

1. Pick two character traits in this passage which you need to cultivate. Is it easier to think of what others should do?
2. Choose a situation in which one person should forgive another. Are there some people you should be forgiving right now? Why is it hard sometimes?
3. Does v. 16 mean that folk songs should be excluded from Christian worship?
4. "Colossians 3:17 teaches that worldly amusements are wrong." True or false? Why?
5. What can you do in your community to provide wholesome recreation?

ADDITIONAL RESEARCH

1. Which verse in I Corinthians 13 is closest to v. 12?
2. Is there a difference between being commanded to "put on" kindness (v. 12) and becoming "rooted and built up in him" (2:7)?
3. How is "Let the word of Christ dwell in you richly" related to our union with Christ?
4. Who are the *elect of God* (v. 12)?

STUDY 9: COLOSSIANS 3:18—4:1

BASIC INFORMATION

1. List the different categories of people to whom Paul gives advice.

2. In what verses are the words *Lord* or *Master* found?

3. Match the persons in the column on the left with the recipients of the instructions in the column on the right:

masters	submit as it is fit
husbands	be just and equal
wives	be not bitter
children	obey to be well pleasing
fathers	provoke not

4. What motivation should Christians cultivate according to v. 23?

DISCUSSION AND APPLICATION

1. Is there a reason why each commandment in this passage is assigned to particular persons?

2. Why does the New Testament in several instances say that wives should *submit* to their husbands, but never does it say that they ought to *obey* their mates? Is this an important distinction or is it just nit-picking?

3. Why do wives often quote v. 19 and husbands usually quote v. 18, when it should be the other way around? Give examples of how these two verses can be applied.

4. How might parents treat their children unjustly?

5. Do you know of cases in which people were penalized for doing right (v. 25)?

6. How do master and slave relationships of that time compare to present day labor and management?

7. How does the instruction in vss. 18–19 affect dating for Christians:

   (a) Date only those you could totally submit to or love.

(b) Only go steady with those you could totally submit to or love.
(c) Date only Christians.
(d) Don't date at all.

ADDITIONAL RESEARCH

1. Does this passage justify the system of slavery, or does it make the best of the situation in which these churches found themselves?
2. Does this chapter prove that there are moral absolutes or that right and wrong are relative to the situation?
3. Outline some principles for labor and management disputes from this passage.

STUDY 10: COLOSSIANS 4:2–18

BASIC INFORMATION

1. What are Paul's prayer requests in vss. 2–6?
2. Compare several translations of v. 4. Does this verse imply that Paul may have been afraid to witness for Christ occasionally?
3. What does it mean to be *redeeming the time* (v. 5)?
4. What do vss. 7–18 reveal about the early church?

DISCUSSION AND APPLICATION

1. How can Christians be more consistent in their prayer lives?
2. How can you personally use your time more efficiently?
3. Recall a time when you were afraid to witness

for Christ or to let people know that you were a Christian. Did you excuse your action or were you sorry for it and ask God for help?

4. If you were to take its instruction seriously, how would v. 6 affect the following situations:
   (a) You are returning an item, which was misrepresented by the salesman, to the store.
   (b) As a member of a nominating committee you are asking someone to run for an office.
   (c) You are on the phone listening to a neighbor who is criticizing someone.

5. What are some implications of vss. 7–18 which could enhance the warmth and fellowship in your local church?

ADDITIONAL RESEARCH

1. Choose one or two names mentioned in this passage and find other references to them in the New Testament. Now write a brief biographical sketch of each.

2. Analyze Paul's personality from the standpoint of vss. 7–18.

3. What does v. 16 reveal about the epistle to the Colossians and the epistle to the Ephesians?

4. Is this the same Onesimus (v. 9) as is mentioned in the book of Philemon?

REFLECTIONS ON COLOSSIANS

1. What occasion prompted the writing of Colossians? What are the Prison Epistles? Is Colossians one of them?

2. Give a title or heading to each of the Scripture passages in these ten studies.

3. How is the life in Christ different from obeying a list of commandments? Explain what it means to be "in union with Christ" and how this relates to the doctrine of sanctification.

4. Recount the aspects of Christ which the book of Colossians stresses. Note chapter one especially. Someone has said that the theme of this book is—the pre-eminence of Christ. Can you trace this emphasis through all of the chapters?

5. Summarize the instructions in this book for family and business situations.

6. Name one or two ways your habits or attitudes are changing because of this study.

7. What false teachings should the Christian avoid according to this book?

7

II TIMOTHY

Chapters 1—4

STUDY 1: II TIMOTHY 1:1–8

BASIC INFORMATION

1. For whom is the peace of God intended?
2. What is the promise found in Christ?
3. Who had tears according to this passage?
4. *Unfeigned faith* means _____.
5. How many commands are given to Timothy here?
6. Can you find evidence that Paul is in prison?

DISCUSSION AND APPLICATION

1. Who do you know who has *unfeigned faith*?
2. What advice is there for today's mothers and grandmothers who cherish praise such as Timothy's loved ones received in this passage?
3. How can we "stir up the gift of God"?
4. Does the church have a responsibility to provide Christian education or is this primarily the task of the home?

5. What admonition could be given to an unfaithful Christian from this study?
6. What principles of mental health are found in v. 7?
7. How do Christians today display that they are ashamed of Jesus?
8. Was there a time last week when you did not experience the peace of God (v. 2)?

ADDITIONAL RESEARCH

1. Define *grace*, *mercy*, and *peace*.
2. What other verses in the New Testament letters note longing and tears as in v. 4?
3. How is "the gift of God" related to the "putting on of my hands"?
4. In what way was Paul a prisoner? In what way was he not a prisoner? How can a person on a hospital bed be free?

STUDY 2: II TIMOTHY 1:9–18

BASIC INFORMATION

1. According to v. 9 how has God saved people?
2. Why isn't Paul ashamed of being a prisoner?
3. To what task was Paul appointed?
4. Who deserted Paul?
5. How did Onesiphorus help Paul?

DISCUSSION AND APPLICATION

1. "God had plans for our lives before the world was created according to v. 9." Do you agree or disagree? Why?

2. What help does v. 12 give to a Christian with problems?

3. "Paul's purpose in writing this letter was to encourage Timothy to grow in his Christian life." Find evidence to support this statement.

4. Which of these men could identify with v. 12 and 1:8:

   (a) Jimmy Hoffa
   (b) Father Daniel Berrigan
   (c) Richard Wurmbrand
   (d) Dietrich Bonhoeffer
   (e) John Huss

5. Who in your church or community needs the encouragement this passage provides? How can you communicate it to them?

ADDITIONAL RESEARCH

1. Look up the words *call* and *calling* in a concordance. To what do they usually refer?

2. Verses eight and nine are actually part of the same sentence. What would be a better way to divide chapter one and still maintain two studies?

3. Make a time line of events in the life of a Christian by listing the items recorded in vss. 9–10. Would a chronological sequence have a different order of events?

4. Does v. 12 relate to the idea of eternal security?

5. Can you find other references in the New Testament to the people mentioned in this chapter?

STUDY 3: II TIMOTHY 2:1–13

BASIC INFORMATION

1. What two commands are given in vss. 1–2?
2. How does Paul describe the word of God in v. 9?
3. What names does modern society give the three occupations which Paul uses in this passage to illustrate aspects of the Christian life? What do all three have in common?
4. List all of the facts which this passage reveals about the person and work of Jesus.

DISCUSSION AND APPLICATION

1. Is there some teaching in your church that you could be doing (cf. v. 2)?
2. List the names of a soldier, an athlete, and a manual laborer who would be examples of Paul's instructions.
3. What does it mean for Paul to endure all things on behalf of other Christians in v. 10?
4. Verse seven implies that Jesus is active in people's everyday lives. Relate a situation in which you need the Lord's help today.
5. Someone might suggest that the theme of these verses is—be strong. Choose several verses which support or refute this interpretation.

ADDITIONAL RESEARCH

1. How does the clause "the word of God is not bound" (v. 9) relate to the inspiration of the Bible? How is v. 2 related to inspiration?
2. To whom is Paul referring when he speaks of the elect (v. 10)?
3. Are verses twelve and thirteen contradictory?

How would Paul reconcile these two statements if you had the opportunity to speak with him?

4. Describe the eternal glory which the faithful Christian can anticipate (vss. 10–12).

STUDY 4: II TIMOTHY 2:14–26

BASIC INFORMATION

1. The same problem is dealt with in vss. 14, 16, 23. What is it?
2. Restate v. 15 in your own words.
3. What names or descriptions of a Christian can you find in vss. 15, 21, 22, 24?
4. What does "youthful lusts" (v. 22) have to do with "vessels of gold and of silver" (v. 20)?
5. What does v. 25 reveal about God's activity in the world?

DISCUSSION AND APPLICATION

1. Read v. 15 again. Could you be more faithful in studying God's Word privately, for Sunday school, at weekly prayer meeting, or at neighborhood Bible study?
2. What work or office could you perform in the church toward becoming an unashamed servant of Christ?
3. What advice does v. 19 give to believers?
4. Can you think of some beautiful home or mansion which would illustrate Paul's point in v. 20? Describe the decor and the furnishings. How does this illustration relate to good or bad Christians?

5. List some traps which Satan has used on you or on people you know (v. 26).
6. What are some foolish controversies which people debate today (v. 23)?

ADDITIONAL RESEARCH

1. Explain the phrase *before the Lord* (v. 14).
2. How can one be meek (vss. 24–25) and still practice forthrightness (v. 14)?
3. What does *word of truth* (v. 15) have to do with the Bible?
4. What is the foundation to which Paul refers in v. 19?
5. What is Paul's source for the two quotations in v. 19?

STUDY 5: II TIMOTHY 3

BASIC INFORMATION

1. What does Paul say about the last days in v. 1?
2. List the characteristics of evil men mentioned in this passage.
3. List the characteristics mentioned in this chapter which evil men do not possess.
4. What verse in chapter one is related to v. 15 in chapter three?
5. How do vss. 16–17 relate to the rest of the chapter?

DISCUSSION AND APPLICATION

1. How does v. 8 relate to psychopathic behavior?
2. What description of a Christian does Paul give in

verses twelve and seventeen? How could you change your life style to match this description?

3. How does the deception in v. 13 relate to v. 7 and 2:23? Name some religious groups or individuals who may be subject to the prohibition mentioned in v. 7. Defend your idea. Do the other sins mentioned in chapter three apply to these groups or to others?

4. Can you think of some church problem which would be eased if v. 16 were taken seriously? How could your attitude or actions be changed by this verse?

5. Paul says of his trials that "out of them all the Lord delivered me" (v. 11). Can you name some incident in which you, too, came to a similar inner conviction?

6. Are there people whom God has used to teach you the Scriptures (v. 15)? Who could you teach?

7. "This chapter, especially v. 13, teaches that the world is getting worse." True or false? Why?

8. Paul had a host of friends throughout the area. Does this suggest that church members should be active in regional denominational work? Does this encourage broader fellowship outside of the local church? Or is this passage unrelated to these concerns?

ADDITIONAL RESEARCH

1. Does v. 10 represent pride?
2. Find the passage in Acts which is related to v. 11.
3. Does v. 16 refer to the whole Bible? Prove your point.
4. Who are Jannes and Jambres (vss. 8–9)?

STUDY 6: II TIMOTHY 4

BASIC INFORMATION

1. What advice does Paul give Timothy in vss. 1–2?
2. Make a list of the commands given to Timothy which apply to Christians today.
3. Who were the people whom Paul praised? Who received criticism?
4. Outline this passage into at least three paragraphs by finding the verse where each new subject begins.

DISCUSSION AND APPLICATION

1. How could v. 1 be used to witness to a non-Christian?
2. Is v. 8 promoting selfishness by promising a crown as a reward for doing good?
3. Have you had an experience similar to v. 17? Do you know someone else who has?
4. How can v. 18 encourage someone with problems? Could it become an answer which might seem too easy?
5. Are there people you could bring to church? Is v. 11 helpful for encouraging church members to invite the unchurched, or is it unrelated to this subject?

ADDITIONAL RESEARCH

1. Do vss. 3–4 tell why it is important for Christians to have specific Scriptures for testing truth and falsehood?
2. What does v. 11 add to the situation in Acts 15:36–40?
3. What information concerning the second com-

ing of Christ do verses one and eight provide? Can you find other verses related to this?

4. What is the meaning of "I was delivered out of the mouth of the lion" (v. 17)?

5. What insight does this chapter give into Paul's last experiences and emotions?

REFLECTIONS ON II TIMOTHY

1. What is the instruction of II Timothy regarding the revelation and inspiration of the Bible? What other references in the Old and New Testaments relate to these issues?

2. Paul counsels Timothy in various duties of the Christian life. Pretend that a new Christian has asked your advice on becoming a better church member. What suggestions could you give him from this book of the Bible? How does this advice apply to you?

3. What were the circumstances as Paul wrote this letter? Especially review 1:1–18 and 4:5–21.

4. Summarize how II Timothy relates to these topics:
   (a) family life
   (b) mental health
   (c) the gift of God

5. Did Paul learn from the experience of suffering? Could Paul's experience help suffering people today?

6. What warnings did Paul give against false religions?

7. Why is II Timothy considered to be one of the

Pastoral Epistles? What are the others and how are they related to one another?

8. What does this book tell about the second coming of Christ? How does this material relate to the book of Revelation?

8

PHILEMON

BASIC INFORMATION

1. Who was Philemon?
2. What had Onesimus done?
3. Paul requested that _____.
4. According to this passage, what kind of person was Philemon?
5. How had Onesimus been a blessing to Paul?

DISCUSSION AND APPLICATION

1. If the person who introduced you to Christ wrote a letter of reference to another church, what would he say? Would he commend your growth in Christ? What might he suggest for your further growth?
2. Which best typifies Paul's efforts on behalf of Onesimus:
   (a) lawyer
   (b) ambassador

(c) labor-management mediator

(d) umpire

3. Can you surmise why Philemon might not have carried out Paul's wishes? Is there some reason why he should not have?

4. How does Christian fellowship affect employer-employee relationships today? Should coffee breaks be taken separately? How should fellowship affect overtime work and pay? Vacations?

5. Paul was detained and kept in custody by the Roman authorities. How do we sometimes imprison our friends, acquaintances, and family members? Is it understandable that they sometimes shun our influence?

6. If Philemon were following Biblical instructions such as Mark 9:35 and Romans 12:10, would he have traded places with Onesimus?

7. If Philemon were on the verge of bankruptcy, would that affect how he might treat Onesimus?

8. What would Paul have done if Philemon had disregarded v. 17? What would you have done? How have you handled the most recent instance in which someone went against your wishes? If you injure someone, how can you make amends?

ADDITIONAL RESEARCH

1. Is it fair to say that Paul's intercession for Onesimus illustrates Christ's prayers on our behalf? Is it indicative of Jesus' love for us?

2. Does this passage intend to teach anything about slavery? Does it do so accidentally?

REFLECTIONS ON PHILEMON

1. Summarize the main lesson of this letter.

2. Research the occasion, date, and author of this epistle.
3. How does Philemon fit into the chronology of Paul's letters, especially in relation to the epistles to the Colossians and Ephesians?
4. List the practical applications of this letter.
5. Choose the teachings in Philemon which could most significantly change your life.
6. Set up a timetable depicting the progress you expect to make in achieving your choices in question five.

9

JAMES

Chapters 1—5

STUDY 1: JAMES 1:1–8

BASIC INFORMATION

1. What is James's relationship to God?
2. When should Christians be happy according to this passage?
3. List all of the commandments found in vss. 2–5.
4. How can you gain wisdom?
5. What is the role of faith in gaining wisdom?

DISCUSSION AND APPLICATION

1. "It isn't logical to be happy and rejoice when you have big problems." True or false? Why?
2. Who is currently experiencing trouble, as reported in the newspapers? Are you acquainted with people who are having big problems? What struggles are you facing?
3. Are problems and temptations the same thing?
4. What comfort is there in knowing that patience can grow even when you hurt inside?

5. Would we be perfect if we were patient?
6. Give some examples from the Bible to illustrate:
   (a) unanswered prayer
   (b) prayer for wisdom, which God granted
   (c) saints who endured testing
7. Give some contemporary examples for each situation in question four.
8. Can you increase your I.Q. through prayer?

ADDITIONAL RESEARCH

1. To whom was James writing?
2. Why does v. 5 follow v. 4? How are they related to each other?
3. Who were the *twelve tribes* in v. 1? How is this term related to the Diaspora?

STUDY 2: JAMES 1:9–18

BASIC INFORMATION

1. Contrast the rich and the poor in this passage by listing their differences.
2. How is the crown described in v. 12? Imagine that you are writing a want ad for this crown. What would you write?
3. What is another way of saying: "Then when lust hath conceived, it bringeth forth sin"?
4. What did God do for Christians by means of the word of truth (v. 18)?

DISCUSSION AND APPLICATION

1. Does this passage condemn wealth and glorify poverty?

2. Should the poor be proud of their condition according to v. 9? Should we try to be poor?

3. Can you recall an incident in the Bible in which someone was tempted and then yielded to that temptation? Can you share an example from your life?

4. From your own experience with temptation, what hints can you give which would help someone else? What help is found in these verses?

5. If someone in your group or circle of acquaintances were facing a real struggle, where could they go to find help?

ADDITIONAL RESEARCH

1. Is v. 13 an illustration of how men try to "pass the buck"? List other excuses given for yielding to temptation. Find Bible verses which relate to each of these excuses.

2. In v. 17 what information is given concerning the nature of God? List the attributes of God referred to in this verse.

3. How do *the word of truth* (v. 18) and *the word* (1:22) compare? Are they the same? How do they relate to the *words* of the Bible? Find other New Testament passages where these phrases are discussed.

4. Define *firstfruits* (v. 18), *temptation* (v. 12), and *lust* (vss. 14–15).

STUDY 3: JAMES 1:19–27

BASIC INFORMATION

1. What is James's instruction on anger:
   (a) We should be quick to hear.
   (b) We should be quick to speak.
   (c) We should be slow to anger.
   (d) Man's anger usually achieves God's standard of right and wrong.
2. Rewrite v. 21 in your own words.
3. Why is it foolish for a man to disobey God according to this passage?
4. How should Christians deal with the things of the world?

DISCUSSION AND APPLICATION

1. How does anger injure people?
2. Can you recall an incident in which you could have handled your anger differently?
3. How can a high school sophomore live up to v. 22? A young mother of two children living in the suburbs of a big city? A father of five children living in the ghetto?
4. "I think it is impossible for a person who tries to obey laws to feel free." How would the writer of v. 25 react to this statement?
5. In connection with 1:27, list some ways we can help others today.

ADDITIONAL RESEARCH

1. Reread the verses where the following figures of speech are used and then explain each one:
   (a) mirror
   (b) bridle
   (c) tree graft

2. How does v. 27 compare and contrast to the "social gospel"? Who started the social gospel? How does it contrast to a soul-winning emphasis in witnessing for Christ?
3. Does the vain or worthless religion in v. 26 mean that such people will not go to heaven?
4. Define *world* (v. 27) and *law of liberty* (v. 25).

STUDY 4: JAMES 2:1–9

BASIC INFORMATION

1. Explain James's description of Jesus in v. 1.
2. God chose a certain kind of people to possess the kingdom. Describe them.
3. How were the rich people treating the poor in this passage?
4. State the main idea in this passage.
5. What chapter in the gospel of Luke deals with this topic? What verse in Matthew's Sermon on the Mount is similar?

DISCUSSION AND APPLICATION

1. Is the intent of v. 3 that we should always give first place to poor people?
2. Would you act differently if the president of a large corporation came to your home for dinner than if a janitor or construction worker came? What does this passage teach concerning your behavior in such situations?
3. What prejudices in your life does this passage reveal? Are there other biases which you have that are not mentioned here? What steps can you take to deal with these?

4. "A businessman would find it impossible to obey this passage literally." True or false? Why?
5. Would James favor the breakdown of the large corporations in our country?

ADDITIONAL RESEARCH

1. Which of the following topics are relevant to this passage:
   (a) predestination
   (b) racial prejudice
   (c) wrong attitudes toward wealth
   (d) none of the above
2. Formulate a prayer from what this study teaches.
3. Can you recall a story in fiction which illustrates the main idea of this passage?

STUDY 5: JAMES 2:10–26

BASIC INFORMATION

1. Will breaking a minor law make us guilty before God?
2. According to this passage, what should we do if someone has no clothes or no food?
3. Without works faith is _____.
4. Do the demons believe in God?
5. How is faith made perfect?
6. Put v. 26 into your own words.

DISCUSSION AND APPLICATION

1. Does the absence of good deeds prove that a

professing Christian is a phony? Is this different than being a hypocrite?

2. Do you know someone who has practiced helping the less fortunate?

3. Do you agree or disagree with this statement: "If you don't live according to God's will, then there is a basis to doubt whether you really have faith."

4. Someone has suggested that we *are* what we *do*. How does that idea relate to this passage? If it is true, what are you *doing* at church, at work, at home, or at recreation which reveals what you *are*?

5. "In Romans 4:1–5 Paul looks at a subject from God's viewpoint as Judge. In James 2, James considers the same topic from the human standpoint of the servant who must decide how he will live his life. Thus he is opposing the idea that believers can do wrong if they please." What is your reaction to this statement?

ADDITIONAL RESEARCH

1. How do you reconcile Ephesians 2:8–10 with v. 24?

2. Make a list of benevolent programs and organizations which Bible-believing Christians have promoted in the last 100 years.

3. What does v. 19 teach about demons?

4. Look up the references to Abraham and Rahab in the Old Testament to gain some new understanding of their situations.

STUDY 6: JAMES 3:1–12

BASIC INFORMATION

1. What does a rudder have in common with a tongue in this passage? How is a wild animal similar to the tongue?
2. What does control over the tongue indicate according to this passage?
3. What is strange about the potential of the tongue according to vss. 8–9? Can you think of another word for *strange* in the preceding question?
4. Choose one word to summarize the subject of this passage.
5. How is chapter three related to chapter two?

DISCUSSION AND APPLICATION

1. List as many sins of the tongue as possible.
2. Which one of these sins in question must you guard against most of all? Is it a temptation now to change the subject and think of someone else's shortcomings?
3. Does v. 2 imply that a few people might be able to control their tongues perfectly?
4. What might you pray as a result of this study?
5. "I see so many church members who gossip. Therefore I don't want to have anything to do with the church." What is your reaction to this sentiment?

ADDITIONAL RESEARCH

1. Does the mouth say both good and bad things? If so, is the illustration of a fountain (v. 11) inappropriate?
2. Write a dialogue illustrating v. 6.

3. How do you distinguish between the following sins of the tongue:

   (a) lying
   (b) gossiping
   (c) backbiting

4. What other figures could be used to illustrate the power of the tongue in addition to those mentioned in this chapter? Can you find similar metaphors in literature?

STUDY 7: JAMES 3:13–18

BASIC INFORMATION

1. How does wisdom relate to overcoming temptation?

2. What two viewpoints are contrasted in v. 15 and v. 18?

3. Rewrite v. 17 in your own words.

4. Which of the following topics are alluded to in this passage:

   (a) wisdom
   (b) adultery
   (c) pride
   (d) backbiting

DISCUSSION AND APPLICATION

1. How does James caution against bragging? Why do you think James felt as he did?

2. "It is ridiculous for a person to be nice to someone who has deliberately gossiped about him." Do you agree or disagree? How does this passage relate to this statement?

3. Can you think of a recent situation in which the message of v. 18 would have helped solve the problem?
4. How can righteousness be practiced by a government? How can a church practice righteousness by ministering to the needy in its community?
5. What is true wisdom?

ADDITIONAL RESEARCH

1. Distinguish between the items in the following pairs: jealousy and envy, pride and selfishness, and courtesy and gentleness.
2. How is v. 15 related to v. 18? That is, how does one lead into the other?
3. How does the book of Proverbs serve as a background to this passage? Find passages in Proverbs which deal with wisdom and righteousness.

STUDY 8: JAMES 4:1–12

BASIC INFORMATION

1. What causes conflict according to this passage?
2. What can injure one's prayer life?
3. Why is a friend of the world God's enemy? Cf. I John 2:15–17.
4. How can a person repent of worldliness and the desire for material things?
5. Can you find at least five injunctions which relate to repentance?
6. Why should we not judge each other?

DISCUSSION AND APPLICATION

1. Which one of the following personalities best illustrates vss. 1–3:
   (a) Napoleon
   (b) Hitler
   (c) Marilyn Monroe
   (d) Grandma Moses
2. How can you help a young person who is struggling with unholy desires?
3. Describe the worldly person.
4. "As far as criticism is concerned, it's one thing if they're criticizing someone else, but it's another when they're talking about me." What is your reaction to this attitude?

ADDITIONAL RESEARCH

1. "Lust refers only to physical desires." Is this true or false? Why?
2. Relate v. 4 to Ezekiel 23 and the book of Hosea.
3. What do the New Testament names *the adversary* and *the father of lies* reveal about Satan? What other names is he given in the Bible?
4. How is this passage related to the lordship of Christ? Cf. Romans 12:1–2.
5. Compare other New Testament references to judging one another.

STUDY 9: JAMES 4:13—5:6

BASIC INFORMATION

1. What is the occupation of the people in vss. 13–17?

2. How is our life like a vapor?
3. "If there is a good excuse, it is all right to know what to do and not to do it." Find a verse that relates to this statement.
4. What can happen to one's riches according to this passage?
5. Restate v. 13 in your own words. Exactly what is James saying?

DISCUSSION AND APPLICATION

1. In v. 13, does James mean it is wrong to plan to go to another city for a year to conduct business?
2. If you knew that you were going to die tomorrow at this time, what would you do in the remaining twenty-four hours?
3. Why don't people do the right (v. 17)? What are our excuses or rationalizations for gossip, lust, anger, covetousness? What are your excuses?
4. Do you know some rich people who fit the description in vss. 1–6? Do you know some who do not?
5. What are some events which could destroy the value of stocks, bonds, savings deposits, real estate investments, and even money hidden in the ground?
6. Do many nations have a system in which a minority of people possess the majority of the wealth? What attitude should a Christian have toward this system? What should be done about it?

ADDITIONAL RESEARCH

1. Is v. 17 intended to be a definition of sin?
2. Which Old Testament prophet parallels the mood of this passage?

3. Does v. 6 imply that the innocent man should not resist evil actions?

STUDY 10: JAMES 5:7–20

BASIC INFORMATION

1. What character trait is recommended for awaiting Christ's return?
2. What does the story of Job teach according to this passage?
3. Explain verses nine and twelve.
4. What promises are given in vss. 15–18?
5. How did the early church help members with their problems?

DISCUSSION AND APPLICATION

1. How can church members help one another today? How can church members heal one another's wounds? What can your Bible study group do?
2. To what extent should we obey the command to confess our faults to one another?
3. Who do you know who has a mature prayer life? How can you improve yours?
4. How does the fact that Elijah had human weaknesses relate to our situation today?
5. How can you cultivate the virtue of patience?

ADDITIONAL RESEARCH

1. What does the New Testament teach about sickness and healing? How can we obtain healing? Is it always possible?

2. How does v. 12 fit into its context?
3. Is there evidence in the book of Job that Job was not always patient?
4. Which Old Testament saints manifested a good prayer life?

REFLECTIONS ON JAMES

1. What are some of the sins which James warns against?
2. List several suggestions which he offers to overcome temptation.
3. Why isn't James afraid that he might be accused of preaching "social gospel"? Why does he stress exercising mercy toward non-Christians?
4. How does James portray who Satan is and what he does?
5. What do good works have to do with faith?
6. What is the root cause for conflict and wars?
7. Find the details which James chooses to describe the activities of a healthy church and the interaction amongst its church members.
8. In a nutshell, what is James's conception of prayer?
9. How does the book of James differ in background and context from the book of Galatians?
10. What happened to James later in life?

10

I PETER

Chapters 1—5

STUDY 1: I PETER 1:1–9

BASIC INFORMATION

1. To whom did Peter address his letter?
2. What had God done for these people?
3. How does a *lively hope* relate to the resurrection?
4. Why can suffering Christians rejoice?
5. What is the result of a genuine faith?

DISCUSSION AND APPLICATION

1. How can the description of the Christian's inheritance (v. 4) give encouragement to the afflicted? Does it help you with your problems? Why or why not?
2. How do vss. 6–9 assist:
   (a) a person with overwhelming financial problems
   (b) a divorcee

    (c) a parent with a problem teen-ager (or vice versa)

    (d) a seriously ill person

3. Do you know someone who endured great testing and came to love the Lord more and to rejoice greatly (v. 8)?

4. How is the Christian's faith "tried by fire" today?

5. What difference does the indwelling Christ cause in your biggest problem right now?

ADDITIONAL RESEARCH

1. Explain the "sprinkling of the blood of Jesus Christ" (v. 2). How is this related to the doctrine of justification? Baptism?

2. Where else in the New Testament is sanctification related to the Holy Spirit? What is the role of the Spirit of God in the Christian's spiritual growth?

3. Is the context of this letter the persecution of the early church by Rome? If so, is it unfair to apply the idea of affliction in this passage to modern financial problems and physical illnesses?

STUDY 2: I PETER 1:10–25

BASIC INFORMATION

1. What stirred the prophets' wonder?

2. According to vss. 11–12 the Holy Spirit_____.

3. Describe the obedient children of God.

4. What is Peter's instruction to Christians concerning their minds?
5. Why is the blood of Christ precious?
6. What contrast is used to show that the word of God is abiding?
7. In one or two sentences, summarize Peter's call to holiness in vss. 13–16.

DISCUSSION AND APPLICATION

1. What personal insights does this passage offer regarding:
   (a) How a Christian should act.
   (b) How we can obtain power to do God's will.
   (c) How your life would change if you considered holiness more seriously.
2. What does the concept of the holiness of God involve? What does it mean for Christians to be holy?
3. What does it mean to be born again? How is this related to the idea of being redeemed by Christ's blood? Who do you know who gives evidence of being born again? Do you feel that you are born again?
4. List some acts today which might originate in lusts or passions (v. 14).
5. Take time to pray. Ask God for help in the areas being considered in this study.

ADDITIONAL RESEARCH

1. Name some of the prophets referred to in v. 10.
2. What information does this passage offer regarding angels (v. 12)?
3. Show how these are logically interrelated:
   (a) love for the brethren

(b) born anew
(c) the living and abiding Word of God

STUDY 3: I PETER 2:1–12

BASIC INFORMATION

1. What should Christians not do?
2. Match the phrases in the column on the left with the references in the column on the right:

   "newborn babes"   Jesus Christ
   "living stone"   Christians
   "spiritual house"   unbelievers
   "holy priesthood"   none of these
   "malice"

3. Why do people stumble (v. 8)? Consult newer translations.

DISCUSSION AND APPLICATION

1. "Many Christians are hypocrites." Does it help to answer such accusations by explaining that believers are not born into perfection, but must grow in the same way babies grow?
2. In this chapter reference is made to the idea that all believers are priests (verses five and nine). What are the implications of this doctrine in regard to:
   (a) prayer
   (b) freedom of conscience
   (c) separation of church and state
   (d) local church government
3. "Jesus Christ is a living stone." How does this statement help people who are tempted to sin or who have great worries pressing down on them?

4. In relation to v. 12, how can your life be a better witness? What should you avoid in the next twenty-four hours which could be a harmful witness?
5. "I Peter 2:9 destroys the argument of people who justify their evil actions on the basis of their upbringing." True or false? Why?

ADDITIONAL RESEARCH

1. What is the Old Testament context for vss. 6–8?
2. In what other New Testament references is *light* given the connotation of v. 9?
3. Find the Old Testament reference of v. 10. What play on words is used?
4. What else can you discover about the Biblical portrayal of the judgment day?

STUDY 4: I PETER 2:13–25

BASIC INFORMATION

1. List the duties of a citizen.
2. How should servants relate to their masters?
3. What are Jesus' qualifications as your Savior?
4. What was happening while Jesus was hanging on the cross?
5. Who is the *Shepherd* and *Bishop* of the Christian?

DISCUSSION AND APPLICATION

1. When must a citizen obey the law (v. 13)?
2. What are some laws which you have not always obeyed (v. 13)?
3. How does v. 14 relate to capital punishment?

4. What advice does Peter offer in vss. 16–17 to a youth who wants to "do his own thing"?
5. To which of these groups of people do the regulations of v. 18 apply:
   (a) secretaries
   (b) janitors
   (c) post office employees
   (d) students
6. Imagine that a coworker receives a promotion in your office even though he has fewer qualifications than you. He gets the promotion because he is on better terms with the boss. How does v. 19 help in this situation? If you would adopt a martyr complex, might you be contributing to your own problem?
7. When have you felt like a wandering sheep (v. 25)? What does it mean to you that Jesus is your Shepherd?

ADDITIONAL RESEARCH

1. Could a slave ever expect to be happy in the light of vss. 18–19?
2. Did Peter ever refuse to obey a government official?
3. What is *guile* (v. 22)?
4. What other instruction does the New Testament give to employers and employees?

STUDY 5: I PETER 3:1–7

BASIC INFORMATION

1. Why should wives be *in subjection*?
2. What is the main point in vss. 3–4?

3. Who is admonished to possess a meek and quiet spirit (v. 4)?
4. What promise is contained in v. 6?

DISCUSSION AND APPLICATION

1. What advice could this passage offer to Dagwood and Blondie in one of their latest episodes?
2. Imagine that you were living when this letter was first read by Christian wives. Describe how a wife of that time might relate to her husband, assuming she obeyed vss. 1–2.
3. "Peter's instructions to wives do not depersonalize them or cause them to lose dignity or opportunity for self-fulfillment." True or false? Why?
4. In what ways are women weaker than men? Are they stronger in some ways? If so, how do these differences relate to this passage?
5. List some ways husbands could honor their wives when:
   (a) speaking to her in front of children
   (b) speaking to her in the midst of a group
   (c) allowing or denying her request for new clothes
   (d) helping her around the house
6. If v. 1 is to be taken seriously, how would that affect whom Christian girls should date? Are there similar implications for fellows in v. 7?

ADDITIONAL RESEARCH

1. Is there a difference between *subjection* and *obedience* according to the Bible in a wife's relationship to her husband?
2. What other verses in the New Testament give

instructions to husbands and wives? What passage in Proverbs is related to this topic?

3. Does *heirs together* (v. 7) refer to the *glory* of 5:1?

4. Peter warns that failure to obey these injunctions will affect our prayer life. What other actions does the Bible specify as hindering prayer? Give the references.

STUDY 6: I PETER 3:8–22

BASIC INFORMATION

1. What do the characteristics in v. 8 have in common?

2. What advice do verses ten and twelve provide someone seeking a better prayer life?

3. What reasons does Peter give to prove that it is better to suffer unjustly than to do evil?

4. Which attribute of God was evident as the ark was being made?

5. Where is Jesus now?

DISCUSSION AND APPLICATION

1. List several different types of church problems which vss. 8–9 would help to resolve. How can church members express this compassion for one another more than they do?

2. How can one human being bless another?

3. Which of these individuals have been wrongly accused:
   (a) William Tyndale
   (b) Epicurus
   (c) Richard Nixon
   (d) Joseph Stalin

4. Peter talks about a good conscience in v. 16.

What are some things which cause you to be uneasy?

5. "I Peter 3:18 proves that Jesus was a substitute for sinners, bearing their penalty." True or false? Why?

6. What practical help does this passage give you regarding:
   (a) preaching
   (b) fear
   (c) righteousness

ADDITIONAL RESEARCH

1. Is it true that the Old Testament promises that prosperity will result from moral living, and the New Testament promises spiritual blessings? Does v. 10 promise good things for the obedient? Should we expect only good fortune if we live morally?

2. Do v. 15 and Luke 21:14–15 refer to different situations? If so, what is the difference?

3. Explain vss. 19–20. Are they related to Ephesians 4:9–10?

4. How does this passage relate to the following topics:
   (a) the "intermediate state"
   (b) the legal aspects of the atonement
   (c) baptism
   (d) the kingly office of Jesus

STUDY 7: I PETER 4

BASIC INFORMATION

1. List the sins commonly found among non-Christians according to this passage.

2. Which verses refer to Christ's second coming?

3. What does 3:17 reveal about the believer's judgment, and v. 5 reveal about the judgment of sinners?
4. How many instructions can you find relating to love?
5. What do verses eleven and nineteen reveal about the nature of God?

DISCUSSION AND APPLICATION

1. How does Christ's return inject urgency into our Christian service? How does it encourage people with problems?
2. What gifts have you received (v. 10)? Could you make use of them more than you have?
3. Have you ever been able to rejoice at fiery trials (v. 13)? Do you know of some people who have?
4. What information in this chapter should challenge non-Christians to turn to Christ? What can you share with a friend who is searching to become a Christian?
5. Which of the following are examples of God's judgment on people:
   (a) the United States Civil War
   (b) the fall of ancient Rome
   (c) Watergate
   (d) the plagues in the Middle Ages
   (e) recent tornadoes and floods
6. Does this chapter teach a legalistic approach to ethics or does it ground right and wrong in the fulfillment of God's will in the individual?

ADDITIONAL RESEARCH

1. What ethics can you find in this passage?
2. Explain v. 1.
3. How are vss. 10–11 related to I Corinthians 12 and 14?

4. Review all of the passages in I Peter relating to suffering. Can you infer from these passages the troubles these people were facing?

STUDY 8: I PETER 5

BASIC INFORMATION

1. How many different Christian motives can you find in vss. 1–6?
2. How are elders cautioned not to lead the flock of God?
3. Describe the devil as he is presented in this passage.
4. How can we overcome the devil?
5. What is the Christians' hope?

DISCUSSION AND APPLICATION

1. How has God used your pastor to feed your church (v. 2)?
2. How can a pastor be a leader, yet not a dictator (v. 2)? Does this sometimes depend upon which side you are on?
3. Which church leaders today are like the elders of v. 2?
4. What are some anxieties which Americans could leave to God (v. 7)?
5. List several practical steps one can take if he is determined to overcome each of these temptations:
   (a) temper
   (b) covetousness
   (c) discouragement
   (d) lust
6. If God opposes the proud and helps the humble,

how can you change your attitudes to qualify for His assistance?

7. Have you ever felt the devil's presence? What does the Bible promise concerning overcoming him? Can we blame the devil for our sins?

ADDITIONAL RESEARCH

1. How does the Bible depict Satan's origin, appearance, methods, helpers, and final end?
2. What does it mean for a Christian to be *sober* (v. 8)?
3. Did Peter write this book?
4. Compose a benediction based on vss. 10–11 in words that reflect our contemporary language and concerns.

REFLECTIONS ON I PETER

1. To whom, when, and why was this letter written?
2. How is I Peter related to II Peter? Discuss authorship, dates, and style.
3. Describe the joys and blessings of a Christian according to this letter.
4. What are our responsibilities at home, at work, and in citizenship according to Peter? How do these instructions compare to what Paul states in some of his letters?
5. What is Peter's image of a Christian who lives according to the proper ethical standards?
6. Tell what you have learned about salvation in these studies. Why do we need it? Who provides it? How is it provided? How does it affect human beings who respond to it?
7. What advice does Peter give pastors?
8. In what way is *suffering* a basic theme in this book?

11

I JOHN

Chapters 1—5

STUDY 1: I John 1:1—2:2

BASIC INFORMATION

1. What was John's evidence that his beliefs were true?
2. Why did John write this letter?
3. If God is light and we walk in darkness, what is the logical conclusion?
4. What does the blood of Jesus accomplish?
5. What should we do if we have sinned?
6. In order to provide forgiveness, Jesus _____.

DISCUSSION AND APPLICATION

1. If you had seen, heard, and touched Jesus repeatedly, would that have taken away your doubts?
2. *Eternal life* in v. 2 means:
   (a) heaven
   (b) forgiveness

(c) Jesus

(d) ethical living

3. I John 1:4–7 gives several characteristics of the healthy Christian life. List them. Does your life reveal them?

4. How might you be tempted at work, at school, or at home to walk in darkness?

5. On the basis of this passage, what could you tell a friend who has a guilt complex?

6. Is it fair to say that Jesus is our lawyer?

7. Someone tells you, "I have found the four basic points of salvation in I John. First is the fact that men sin and need a deliverer (2:1). Second, Jesus died to pay the penalty for our sins (2:2; 1:7). Third, we must confess our sins (1:8–10). Fourth, we must believe in Jesus and we'll be born of God and have eternal life (5:1, 13)." Does this summarize what John was saying in this epistle?

ADDITIONAL RESEARCH

1. By whom, for whom, when, and under what circumstances was this letter written?

2. Explain the words "and shew unto you that eternal life, which was with the Father, and was manifested unto us" (1:2).

3. Was this letter written to Christians or unbelievers? Could some parts apply to both?

4. Why is *propitiation* (2:2) sometimes translated *expiation*? How do the following passages relate to this question: Mark 10:45; Romans 3:25–26; and II Corinthians 5:21?

STUDY 2: I JOHN 2:3–29

BASIC INFORMATION

1. How can we be certain we know Jesus?
2. In whom is God's love completed?
3. What is the new commandment John notes?
4. How does John distinguish between persons of darkness and persons of light?
5. To what age groups does John speak here?
6. How does John describe the world?
7. How do the antichrists act? What do they deny?
8. What does John say about eternal life?

DISCUSSION AND APPLICATION

1. List several of your actions in the last week which indicate that you *know* God in the sense of v. 3. Can you list several actions which indicate that you don't?
2. Do you know someone who is especially loving?
3. List some activities or life styles which illustrate each of the following:
   (a) lust of the flesh
   (b) lust of the eyes
   (c) pride of life
4. John warns against falsehood in this chapter. In every office, barber shop, beauty parlor, locker room, and kitchen there are people who have definite views on religion and life. Recall which of the following philosophies you have heard recently and evaluate them:
   (a) We'll all get to heaven sooner or later.
   (b) As long as it doesn't hurt anybody, it's all right.
   (c) I'm just as good as any church member, so I'll get to heaven anyhow.

(d) I don't think that we should wear religion on our sleeve.

ADDITIONAL RESEARCH

1. How does John use the word *know*? How does this meaning transcend merely recognizing certain facts?
2. What is the difference in the advice John gives to young and old?
3. Explain v. 18.
4. Are *unction* (v. 20) and *anointing* (v. 27) the same?

STUDY 3: I JOHN 3

BASIC INFORMATION

1. Describe God's love toward us.
2. What will we see when Christ appears?
3. What is sin?
4. Describe the person who practices sin according to this passage.
5. Complete the following statement with one of the phrases listed below: "The one who is born of God_____"
   (a) has God's seed remaining in him.
   (b) is a child of God.
   (c) commits sin.
   (d) has heard the message from the beginning.
6. What do murder, lack of compassion, and condemnation of others have in common?
7. What do the following concepts in this passage have in common: confidence, belief, love, and constancy?

DISCUSSION AND APPLICATION

1. What kind of love has the Father showered upon us?

2. How would v. 2 help people in the following situations:
   (a) sorrowing
   (b) sick
   (c) imprisoned
   (d) handicapped
   (e) emotionally disturbed

3. How are you purifying yourself (v. 3)?

4. "Verses eight and nine refer to continuing in sin." Do you agree or disagree? Why?

5. Who are some needy people in your neighborhood you could help (v. 17)?

6. Is John's view of the Christian life too idealistic? Is it impossible to live up to this standard?

7. How do you answer those who object that the prayer promise in v. 22 is too easy?

ADDITIONAL RESEARCH

1. Does v. 15 make everyone a murderer?

2. What is John's conception of *truth* (v. 18)?

3. What doctrine of the Holy Spirit develops in chapters two and three?

STUDY 4: I JOHN 4

BASIC INFORMATION

1. "We should believe every preacher who quotes Bible verses to support his views." True or false according to this passage?

2. What clue distinguishes between true and false religion?
3. How is *the world* described here?
4. "God is love" (v. 16). What implications does John find in this idea?
5. Who has seen God?
6. Who has sent the Son?
7. "God is love" (v. 16). How does that affect our view of the day of judgment?

DISCUSSION AND APPLICATION

1. Recall a time when you were almost snared by a false teaching.
2. Can you prove that John was talking about more than rocks, hills, rivers, and clouds when he referred to *the world*?
3. Does v. 10 imply a reasonable penalty from a holy God or the impulsive act of an unpredictable god?
4. Is it easier to love someone if they love you first? Does it help you love unattractive people if you know that God loved you while you were a sinner?
5. Does the proof in v. 13 increase your assurance of salvation?
6. Should you be more fearful or less fearful of the day of judgment than you are?
7. What would motivate you to be a more gentle and loving person?

ADDITIONAL RESEARCH

1. Does the concept of Jesus Christ *come in the flesh* imply that Jesus is God?
2. Would it be more appropriate to say that *faith* casts out fear (v. 18)?

STUDY 5: I JOHN 5

BASIC INFORMATION

1. What happens to a person who believes in Jesus?
2. "Love overcomes the world." True or false? Give the verse that answers this question.
3. Which divine witnesses testify concerning Jesus?
4. Who makes God a liar?
5. "He that hath the Son_____life." Which modern usage fits the meaning of v. 12:
   (a) *had* (past tense)
   (b) *has* (present tense)
   (c) *will have* (future tense)
6. What prayer promise is given in this chapter?
7. Is committing sin a serious matter?
8. Who is the true God?

DISCUSSION AND APPLICATION

1. "The basic way to become a Christian is to believe. The basic way to give evidence of this is to love God and others." Cite verses from this passage to prove or disprove this statement. How would this statement affect a plumber, an army officer, or a fisherman?
2. If obedience to commandments is stressed, does that make religion legalistic and destroy love as a basic motiviation?
3. Where does eternal life exist:
   (a) in our strong faith
   (b) in the Son
   (c) in great saints
4. Can a person *know*, as well as *hope*, that he is going to heaven?

ADDITIONAL RESEARCH

1. Do the references to *born of God* in I John mean the same as *born again* in John 3:3, 5, 7?
2. What part of v. 7 is omitted in some translations? Should it be omitted?
3. Explain v. 16.
4. Is the *sin* in v. 18 referring to sinning wilfully? Would this interpretation encourage you to yield to temptation occasionally?
5. Does v. 18 refer to the devil? Does this verse prove that a Christian can never become demon possessed?

REFLECTIONS ON I JOHN

1. What were John's circumstances when he wrote this letter?
2. Outline this book by choosing verses which introduce new topics.
3. Does John equate eternal life with moral living? Give evidence to support your answer.
4. What is the logic in saying that if we don't practice morality and truth, we are really not Christians?
5. Some psychologists say that love and hate are closely related. How does that idea relate to I John?
6. How does I John (especially chapter five) increase one's assurance of salvation?
7. Define the following terms as they are used in I John:
   (a) world
   (b) know

(c) love
(d) light
(e) eternal life
(f) abide
(g) born
(h) truth

8. Has your appreciation and use of the Bible improved as a result of these studies? Review the goals of these studies in the introduction. How can you more effectively realize these goals?

12

REVELATION

Chapters 1, 20—22

STUDY 1: REVELATION 1:1–8

BASIC INFORMATION

1. Why was this book written?
2. What promise is given to those who read it?
3. What is Jesus Christ doing for His followers?
4. Which of the following phrases in this passage does not refer to Jesus:
   (a) "Alpha and Omega"
   (b) "cometh with clouds"
   (c) "first begotten of the dead"
   (d) "which is, and which was, and which is to come"
   (e) "Revelation of Jesus Christ"
   (f) "faithful witness"

DISCUSSION AND APPLICATION

1. Is it possible that you will see Jesus returning? Would you wail (v. 7) or be glad?

2. If Jesus is the first and the last, how would that affect your daily worries and cares?
3. "Unto him that loved us, and washed us from our sins in his own blood" (v. 5). How can a person experience this for himself?
4. If Jesus is the prince of the kings of the earth, does that give Him the right to give us orders? Does it give Him the right to be Mao Tse-Tung's boss?

ADDITIONAL RESEARCH

1. What is the significance of "Alpha and Omega, the beginning and the ending"?
2. Why weren't letters sent to more than seven churches?
3. What circumstances brought John to the situation in v. 4?
4. What does the word *Revelation* mean in v. 1? How is it related to the title of this New Testament book? What is the dictionary meaning of this word?

STUDY 2: REVELATION 1:9–20

BASIC INFORMATION

1. Where and when did the events in this passage occur?
2. List the sights and sounds which John saw and heard.
3. How did John react?
4. What keys did this Being have?

5. Can you find verses in this passage which relate to the following topics:
   (a) fainting away
   (b) worship
   (c) the Bible
   (d) a statue
   (e) purgatory
   (f) a musical instrument
   (g) an interview
   (h) a split-level house
   (i) a book on dieting

DISCUSSION AND APPLICATION

1. If John is our companion in tribulation, how does that affect our attitude toward Christians of other denominations, races, or countries? How important is doctrinal agreement in our concept of companionship? Does it bother you that John may have been from a different culture or ethnic background than yourself?
2. How would you have felt if you had been alongside John during this experience?
3. If you had been there with John, would you have gained incentive to face your everyday discouragements and routine?
4. What does this passage say to local churches?
5. What information does this passage provide regarding the revelation and inspiration of the Bible?

ADDITIONAL RESEARCH

1. What does it mean that John was *in the Spirit* on the Lord's day?
2. What is the significance of having the keys of hell and death?
3. Does the *white* in v. 14 symbolize sinlessness?

STUDY 3: REVELATION 20

BASIC INFORMATION

1. What happened to the devil?
2. The first resurrection is composed of what events?
3. Trace Satan's downfall from the time of his release to his final end.
4. What happened to those present at the great white throne judgment?

DISCUSSION AND APPLICATION

1. Cite evidence from your own experience to prove or disprove that Satan is active today.
2. What hope is offered for Christian martyrs? Is there a limit on those who will take part in the first resurrection?
3. What advice does this passage offer a non-Christian?
4. For someone confined to a bed or an elderly shut-in, what does this story offer?
5. Is it wrong to accept Christ just to avoid the judgment?

ADDITIONAL RESEARCH

1. Who will appear before the great white throne judgments?
2. Is the 1000 years in this passage to be understood literally? Do the Old Testament prophecies of the lamb dwelling with the wolf find their fulfillment in these 1000 years?
3. When, in the chronology of things, will the millenium occur?

STUDY 4: REVELATION 21

BASIC INFORMATION

1. What did John see?
2. Who can have his thirst taken away?
3. Who is excluded from this city?
4. Which of the following cannot be found in this city:
   (a) temple
   (b) sun
   (c) liars
   (d) gates

DISCUSSION AND APPLICATION

1. What hope does v. 4 offer a parent grieving the loss of a child?
2. In the light of your present situation, do you wish to quickly reach this place John describes?
3. How does this passage relate to the following situations:
   (a) Teen-agers who become enthralled with ouija boards and seances.
   (b) A politician giving testimony before a congressional hearing answers five questions. He perjures himself with one answer, but no one discovers the falsehood during the man's lifetime.
   (c) A businessman secretly conducts an extramarital affair.
4. Have you had your thirst quenched by the fountain of the water of life? Is your name written in the Lamb's book of life?

ADDITIONAL RESEARCH

1. Will the new heaven and earth described in this passage occur on our planet?

2. Who is the *bride*?
3. Is the description of the city to be understood literally or symbolically?
4. Why doesn't the new Jerusalem need a temple?

STUDY 5: REVELATION 22

BASIC INFORMATION

1. What is significant about the water of life and the tree of life?
2. What becomes of the curse?
3. What becomes of the filthy or unrighteous?
4. Restate in your own words the testimony here concerning how this book is to be treated.
5. What invitation is given here?

DISCUSSION AND APPLICATION

1. How does this chapter relate to today's newspaper headlines? Does it change your outlook on the future?
2. If men are rewarded according to their works (v. 12), is this a deterrent to sin?
3. Why aren't people with an unethical life style concerned about this?
4. "The Spirit and the bride say, Come." What hymns use this concept? Do you feel that this offer is addressed to you? If you do, how do you feel about that? What is your decision?

ADDITIONAL RESEARCH

1. What clarification do other Bible passages give concerning the "river of water of life"?

2. Where in the Old Testament books did the curse originate?
3. Find another instance where John falls down and begins to worship an angel.
4. How many descriptions of Jesus does this chapter provide? What is the origin of each of these?
5. What do vss. 18–19 reveal about Biblical inspiration?

REFLECTIONS ON REVELATION

1. Why was the book of Revelation written?
2. List the three things in these studies which encouraged you most and the three things that challenged you most.
3. Which of the events in these studies have already occurred and which, do you think, are yet to occur?
4. How can you decide what should be interpreted symbolically in these passages?
5. What is your evaluation of the second coming of Christ? When will He return? What school of thought most nearly expresses what you believe?
6. Does the return of Christ inspire people to greater devotion to Him and greater faithfulness to His will? How does this affect you?
7. How can you begin a systematic study of Scripture?